MARCEL PROUST

MODERN MASTERS

MODERN MASTERS

EDITED BY frank kermode

87

marcel
proust

roger shattuck

NEW YORK | THE VIKING PRESS

NOTE ON TEXTS
AND TRANSLATIONS

Four different English-language editions of Proust's novel are available. All carry the title *Remembrance of Things Past*, and in all cases the first six volumes are translated by C. K. Scott Moncrieff:

Modern Library, 7 volumes, 1924–32: final volume translated by Frederick A. Blossom

Random House, 7 volumes in 2, 1932: final volume translated by Frederick A. Blossom

Chatto & Windus, 7 volumes, 1922–70: final volume translated by Andreas Mayor

Vintage Books, 7 volumes, 1971: final volume translated by Andreas Mayor

Because of the multiplicity of English-language editions, and because the original French text of quotations has not been included here, all page references given in parentheses are to the standard French editions of Proust's works. (There is also a seven-volume edition of the novel in Livre de Poche.) The following abbreviations are used:

JS: Jean Santeuil précédé de *Les Plaisirs et les jours*. Paris: Gallimard, Bibliothèque de la Pléiade, 1971.

CSB: *Contre Sainte-Beauve* précédé de *Pastiches et mélanges* et suivi de *Essais et articles*. Paris: Gallimard, Bibliothèque de la Pléiade, 1971.

  I: *A la recherche du temps perdu*. Paris: Gallimard, Bibliothèque de la Pléiade, 1954, tome I.

 II: ———, tome II.

III: ———, tome III.

Translations from Proust quoted in the text are by Roger Shattuck.

CONTENTS

Contents | x

DIAGRAMS

BIOGRAPHICAL NOTE

1871	Proust born July 10. Brother born two years later.
1880	First asthma attack.
1882–90	Studies at Lycée Condorcet. Military service. Brief university study.
1890–1907	Social climbing. Publishes stories and essays in literary reviews and newspapers. Influence of Robert de Montesquiou. *Les Plaisirs et les jours* published in 1896. Discovers Ruskin's work and translates two of his books. Two versions of a novel remain unpublished. Father and mother die (1903, 1905).
1908–13	Intense work on a new draft of his novel; "finished" in 1912. First volume published in 1913. Second in preparation.
1914–22	Constant writing and poor health. World acclaim after the Goncourt Prize is awarded to second volume in 1919. Two more volumes published before Proust dies on November 18, 1922.
1923–27	Appearance of remaining three volumes.

The Work and Its Author

i

Among the handful of genuine classics produced in this century, Marcel Proust's *In Search of Lost Time* is the most oceanic—and the least read. Publishers' sales figures in all countries confirm the latter observation. Let us begin on this bleak terrain and work back gradually to what is compelling and often entertaining in Proust. To ignore what impedes easy access to his work would be foolish. Proust's substantial reputation as an extreme case of something—longwindedness, psychological vivisection, the snobbery of letters, salvation by memory—rests not on wide readership but on a myth of uniqueness defended by a dedicated few. In an era when the significance and the privileged status of the work of art are being cast into doubt, this ultimate monument to the artistic vocation, banked high on all sides by interpretation and biography, refuses to sink back into the sands of time.

OBSTACLES AND INDUCEMENTS

The inordinate length of Proust's novel (3000 pages) goes a long way toward explaining the scarcity of readers. Even Russian novelists usually limit themselves to half that length. Balzac's one-hundred-volume print-out of all French society comes in separate packages; the links between the volumes serve as a special reward for the perservering. The first two sections of Proust's novel, "Combray" and "Swann in Love," can stand separately and have earned many admirers. Yet true believers insist that there is no substitute for the cumulative effect of the whole work. Understandably, many readers hesitate to make the investment of time and attention required to assimilate even a fraction of the whole.

Compounding the challenge of sheer magnitude, there is Proust's style. His transcontinental sentences contribute to the appearance of a motionless plot. The original French is no easier than the translations. How can one follow a story line (if there really is one) through such labyrinthine prose? Furthermore, Proust originally planned to publish his novel in two compact volumes in rapid succession. The five-year interval of war that occurred after the appearance of the first volume and the tremendous expansion of the text it led to, forced him to change his plans. Published between 1913 and 1927 in multiple installments, the *Search* is basically divided into seven volumes of very unequal length. For a decade and a half critics tried to judge the whole from a few parts. As a result, Proust had to serve as the sole qualified guide to his own uncompleted work. Endless letters, several newspaper interviews, and over a hundred pages in his last volume are devoted to rebutting his critics and explaining how he was constructing the vast edifice. The opening sections, he insists, give a distorted impression of the whole. Everything hangs on the conclusion. Gradually, Proust's description of his work has been validated by three generations of critics. But for fifteen years his work appeared piecemeal in the face of enormous odds against comprehension. It looks almost like a conspiracy against readers.

These basic circumstances surrounding Proust's work have spawned a set of secondary misunderstandings. Many of them can be traced to remarks by early critics, some of whom were sympathetic. Edmund Wilson, the earliest and most perceptive of American critics, admired Proust's work; yet he called the *Search* "one of the gloomiest books ever written." In this instance his critical acumen failed him. Proust's novel earns its place in literature as a great comic tale, punctuated with smiles and guffaws. Henry James produced a formula that has been well received: "inconceivable boredom associated with the most extreme ecstasy which it is possible to imagine." It is hard to read the sentence as anything but dispraise. The volume of "tributes" a dozen English writers devoted to Proust in 1923 sows even more confusion. Joseph Conrad finds intellectual analysis at its most creative, but "no reverie, no emotion. . . ." Three pages later, George Saintsbury insists on a "constant relapse upon—and sometimes self-restriction to—a sort of dream element." Had they read the same author? Arnold Bennett wrote more in outrage than in tribute and could not excuse "the clumsy centipedalian crawling of the interminable sentences." Then there is Aldous Huxley's description (though not in this same volume) of Proust as a hermaphrodite, toadlike creature spooning his own tepid juice over his face and body. On the centenary of Proust's birth in 1971 *The New York Times Book Review* assigned its front page to the novelist William H. Gass for a discussion of Proust's work. Gass's rancorous article adds little to Bennet's comments.

> . . . there is no special truth in him. . . . Proust writes a careless self-indulgent prose, doesn't he? . . . Epithet follows epithet like tea cakes in flutes of paper. . . .

It is a style that endangers the identity of the self in
its reckless expressions of it.   —*July 11, 1971*

The fact that many of these critics contradict one
another does not discredit them collectively or individ-
ually. But it does mean that we must beware of incom-
prehension and prejudice. The most persistent negative
judgments of Proust can be reduced to two. First,
Proust's work is boring because of slackness in both
style and construction. Second, the moral universe of
Proust's work never breaks free from the attitude of a
spoiled, sickly, adolescent snob born to wealth on the
fringes of high culture and high society. To these criti-
cisms I shall add two more that are less frequently
voiced.

Clausewitz describes war as the continuation of policy
by other means. Like many authors, Proust often treated
writing as a continuation of life by other means. The
word can conquer where the flesh is weak. Having discovered this path, Proust became one of the great mega-
lomaniacs of literature, unwilling (in part because of
his semi-invalid condition in later years) to relinquish
any small hold he could gain over other people by
writing. In his letters he often mixed honey with acid.
He dominated his mother with inter-bedroom memo-
randa and his friends with pitiful pleas for help. He
sought to hypnotize his readers and to command the
world from his sickbed. This sensitive weakling sought
power and won it.

The last stricture is closely related. From Proust's
writings, as from an electric generator, flows a powerful
current always ready to shock not only our morality but
our very sense of humanity. He undermines individual
character as the source of anything coherent or reliable
in our behavior. Love and friendship, honesty and sex-
uality crumble into mockeries of human relationships.
Except for Marcel's immediate family, no one in the
Search escapes the curses of selfishness, self-contempt,

and snobbery. Few grounds for human dignity survive Proust's touch. The inhumanity of artistic creation seems to triumph over everything.

Quite deliberately I have begun with a harsh and seriously distorted version of Proust's stature. Each of the charges could be rebutted and probably disproved. But I feel it is wise not to affirm his innocence but to ask for a far more illuminating verdict: *guilty—but not as charged.* For Proust had the power to modify, as he went along, the laws under which he wrote and under which he asks us to read. Neither the novel form nor "human nature" remains unchanged after he has passed. The problem is to detect and measure the shifts. Snobbery, megalomania, and instability of character do indeed loom large in the world Proust creates. The first task of the critic is to prevent the uninitiated reader from reacting against these elements before he understands how they fit together to make a remarkably coherent work of art.

No single theory or approach will make Proust easily and quickly available to all inquiring minds. The very resistance of his work to simplification and analysis constitutes its most evident general characteristic. Beyond this feature, however, we discover endless contradictions in the *Search.* Walt Whitman lived at peace with the fact that he contradicted himself. He said that he contained multitudes. Proust asks the next question. How much of his multitudinous self can a person be or embody at one time? The first answer is plain common sense: it all depends. It depends on many things, from chance and volition to memory and forgetting. The second answer is categorical. No matter how we go about it, *we cannot be all of ourselves all at once.* Narrow light beams of perception and of recollection illuminate the present and the past in vivid fragments. The clarity of those fragments is sometimes very great. They may even overlap and reinforce one another. However, to summon our entire self into simultaneous existence lies beyond our powers. We live by synechdoche, by cycles of being. More profoundly than any other novelist, Proust perceived this state of things and worked as an economist of the personality. In himself and in others he observed its fluctuations and partial realizations. Through habit and convention we may find security in "the immobility of the things around us" (I, 6). Yet it affords only temporary refuge. We yield with excitement, apprehension, and a deeper sense of existence to the great wheeling motion of experience. On a single page Proust refers to that endless shifting process as both "the secret of the future" and "the darkness we can never penetrate" (II, 67). He also has a word for it: our lot is "intermittence," the only steady state we know.

As in life itself, the scope of action and reflection encountered in the *Search* exceeds the capacity of one mind to hold it all together at one time. Thus the novel embodies and manifests the principle of intermittence: to live means to perceive different and often conflicting aspects of reality. This iridescence never resolves itself completely into a unitive point of view. Accordingly, it is possible to project out of the *Search* itself a series of putative and intermittent authors. Precisely that has happened. The portraitist of an expiring society, the artist of romantic reminiscence, the narrator of the laminated "I," the classicist of formal structure—all these figures are to be found in Proust, approximately in that order of historical occurrence. All are present as discernible components of his vision and his creation. His principle of intermittence anticipates such veerings of critical emphasis. It is in the middle of a literary discussion that his Narrator observes, "*On ne se réalise que successivement*" (III, 380). It really means: one finds, not oneself, but a succession of selves. Similarly, Proust's work is still going on in our gradual discovery of it.[1]

[1] Critical attention to Proust shows no sign of flagging and has begun to dispel the misconceptions and to probe the

THE LIFE OF AN *Enfant Nerveux*

If forced to make the distinction, most of us would indicate a deeper and more lasting interest in people than in works. We ascribe greatness or goodness more readily to an individual person, accountable for the actions of his whole life, than to a deed detached from its context of individual agency and motivation in a person's life. One could with good reason interpret the history of Western civilization as a sustained attempt to divert us toward a concern with good works, both ethical and artistic. Religion and esthetics have developed along curiously parallel paths. Yet fundamentally our attention directs itself toward men and women, their temperaments and their lives. Only a lifetime provides an adequate unit of significance and value. (We have also cultivated a powerful materialist doctrine: the tendency to judge a man not by what he is or does, but by what he *owns*.)

It is not surprising, therefore, that the biography of so curious a figure as Proust should exert a fascination equal to that of his literary work. I suspect that more readers have read through George D. Painter's biography of Proust than have reached the end of the *Search*. Furthermore, Proust's work lies in very close proximity to his life. On two occasions toward the end of the novel, when he supplied a first name for his Narrator-hero, Proust used his own, Marcel (III, 75, 157). Writers' lives are neither holy ground nor useless appendages. Without some knowledge of Proust's biography, we would remain blind to a whole section of countryside surrounding his work and lending meaning to it.

Proust's life began with the Paris Commune of 1871

paradoxes I have mentioned. Among recent critics Gilles Deleuze, Gérard Genette, René Girard, and J.-F. Revel have produced fine studies in French. The books by Leo Bersani and George Stambolian in English maintain a comparable level of discourse. See Short Bibliography, p. 177.

and ended in fame and exhaustion four years after
World War I. In those fifty-one years he lived two
closely interlocking careers. Beginning very early, this
sensitive, gifted young man with something slightly
Middle Eastern about his soft manner and dark look,
carried out a brilliant escape from his bourgeois background and from the professional career expected of
the eldest son of a prominent Paris doctor. He accomp-
lished this feat by ingratiating himself with the wealthy
and sometimes aristocratic families of his schoolmates
at the Lycée Condorcet. By the age of seventeen, exploit-
ing his talents as a mimic and conversationalist, he was
visiting literary salons and learning his way in society.
In his mid-thirties, soon after the death of both his
parents, his first career as a somewhat eccentric man
of the world gave way to another activity: literature.
Up to that point Proust's writing had served his social
ambitions or had been kept hidden. He now reversed
the poles of his existence. For the last fifteen years of
his life, his social connections and his worldliness furnished the raw material of his writing.

It was a shift, never a clean break. Proust claimed
that he wrote parts of his first book at the age of
fourteen (*JS*, 902), and there is little reason to doubt
him. Just a month before he died, suffering terri-
bly and aware of how much remained to be done on
the final volumes of his novel, he got out of bed to go
to a party given by the Comte and Comtesse de Beau-
mont. The overlap of careers was extensive. Nevertheless, the general movement of Proust's life pivots on an
obscure point, somewhere between 1905 and 1909, in
which north and south changed places. He became a
convert—a convert to true faith in himself as the novelist of his own conversion.

Such a schematic version of Proust's life keeps things
simple and clear. It glosses over minor conflicts of fact
and major conflicts of interpretation. There are good
reasons for us to seek a closer knowledge of how Proust

became a convert to his own calling. The most systematic and the least satisfactory explanations of Proust's life are pseudomedical. Son and brother of prominent doctors, Proust was himself a contributor to this line of thought. Inevitably he had heard that the terrors and upheavals of the Commune (his father was almost shot by accident) had affected his mother's pregnancy. Sickly at birth, he nevertheless survived. Nine years later came his first serious attack of asthma; he received all the attention he could want, and his condition stabilized during youth and early manhood. The attacks recurred in his mid-twenties, at about the time he was coming to terms with his homosexuality. Mostly from his own testimony we know that he was prone to hypochondria, voyeurism, and certain forms of sadomasochism. Psychoanalysts have produced resounding terms to apply to the roots of his condition. When Serge Béhar speaks of "infantile neurosis developing into coenesthopathy in the adult," he is affirming a diseased condition of the organic sensation of existence and well-being. Perhaps: but this ground is as treacherous as it is fascinating. And I wonder if the technical vocabulary really improves on the term Proust's family applied to him very early and which he cites frequently in *Jean Santeuil: un enfant nerveux.*

It is significant that all psychological studies of Proust accept his designation of the determining childhood scene: the goodnight kiss described near the opening of the *Search.* But to what extent is it part of Proust's biography? To what extent is it fiction? In the earlier *Jean Santeuil* version of the scene, the little boy revels in the power and freedom he finds when he finally triumphs over his mother's refusal to leave her guests and come to his room to kiss him goodnight. The same scene in the *Search* emphasizes a strong aftertaste of disappointment over the fact that his mother and father give in to his importunings. Their capitulation, the Narrator states, undermines what little will power the boy has to control his moods. No one has gone further than Proust himself in probing the complete significance of this scene. But we cannot for that reason read it unquestioningly as autobiography.[2]

Heredity provides another way of explaining Proust's temperament and behavior. George Painter seems to accept the "fact" of Proust's "hereditary neurasthenia" and calls attention to a similar condition in a paternal aunt who became a recluse. André Maurois lays great emphasis on the mingling of two parental strains: French-Catholic and Jewish. One cannot readily attribute contrasting character traits to these two races or religions as true genetic strains. On the other hand, the marriage did combine two contrasting cultures. In Proust's sensibility one soon detects the jostling opposition between city and country, between cosmopolitan Paris and provincial, semipastoral Illiers/Combray. His father never lost the brusque manners of a village candlemaker's son. Dr. Proust was the first of a long line of farmers and tradesman to leave Illiers. Mme. Proust,

[2] In a volume of provocative psychoanalytic studies, *L'Arbre jusqu'aux racines*, Dominique Fernandez interprets the whole of the *Search*, and this sequence in particular, as an elaborate feint on Proust's part to distract our attention from his jealousy of his younger brother and disappointment in his father, and from the overpowering domination of his mother. Thus, according to Fernandez, Proust masks the true origins of his homosexuality and protects the myth of the happy family. Many of Fernandez' points are persuasive, but he has a distressingly narrow belief in "precise psychological causes" from which all human behavior will "necessarily flow." Those causes reduce a novel to an excrescence of a psychological case history. I cannot acept this tight determinism on any level of life or literature. Proust's novel makes revelations that transcend his particular case and cannot be read back into it. There, in fact, lies the principal justification for calling it a novel. Fernandez also argues that *Jean Santeuil* is a better and more courageous book than the *Search* because it reveals more about Proust's neurosis than the final novel. Though Fernandez argues his premise very resourcefully, his conclusion does not follow.

fifteen years younger than her husband, was the highly educated, art-loving daughter of a wealthy stockbroker. Her brother was a bachelor and ladies' man; her mother had connections in elegant society and in the world of literature and the arts. The tidal movement of the *Search* arises not from a contrast of races or religions but from a geographic and intellectual exchange between city culture and country culture. We see it first in the "two ways" that polarize the child's world of Combray, and later in the contrast between Combray itself and Paris.

Whatever Proust's medical and psychological condition may have been, and whatever his heredity, he found his own path into the Parisian life of *la belle époque*. He had a quick mind, a prodigious memory (especially for poetry), and a hypersensitive discernment of other people's feelings and reactions. Despite frequent illnesses during his teens, he was healthy enough to excel in school, especially in philosophy. The philosophy teacher Darlu, who tutored him privately for a year, made a profound impression on him and introduced him to the idealist analysis of the contrast between appearance and reality. Very early, Proust fixed on reading and literature as the locus of his interests. He apparently experienced puppy love a number of times. In the most intense instance, his parents thwarted his desires for Marie de Benardaky by insisting that she was socially too far beyond his reach. Taking advantage of a law discriminating in favor of the rich and educated, Proust volunteered at eighteen for one year of military service. Though he did not distinguish himself as a soldier, he made several good friends among the other privileged young men and later called that year the happiest of his life.

One of the favorite pastimes in that self-conscious society was a modified game of truth or consequences played by filling in an elegantly printed questionnaire. Some families kept albums containing these questionnaires along with other mementos of their friends and relatives. In Proust's case we have two such documents, one written at thirteen and the other at twenty. Despite the artificial circumstances, Proust's answers furnish two unmatchable probes of these early years of the slow bloomer. Where possible, I quote both sets of answers.

What is for you the greatest unhappiness? To be separated from maman (13). Not to have known my mother and grandmother (20).

In what place would you like to live? In the land of the Ideal, or rather of my ideal (13). In the place where certain things I want would come to pass as if by enchantment—and where tender feelings would always be shared (20).

Your ideal of earthly happiness? To live near all my loved ones, with the charms of nature, lots of books and musical scores, and, not far away, a French theater (13). I'm afraid it isn't high enough, and I'm afraid of destroying it by telling it (20).

For what faults do you have the greatest indulgence? For the private life of geniuses (13). For those I understand (20).

Your principal fault? Not to know how, not to be able, to will something [*vouloir*] (20).

What would you like to be? Myself, as people I admire would like me to be (20).

Your favorite quality in a man? Intelligence, the moral sense (13).

Your favorite quality in a woman? Tenderness [*douceur*], naturalness, intelligence (13).

Your favorite occupation? Reading; daydreaming; poetry (13). Loving (20).

Your present state of mind? Annoyance [*ennui*] over having thought about myself to answer all these questions (20).

Even for the era these are precocious answers, steeped in literary attitudes, and displaying the capacity to speak the truth within certain limits of coyness and insecurity. No bumbler wrote these apothegmatic lines.

At twenty this young sensitive had to face the painful

question of what he would do with himself. For close to fifteen years he temporized and spent his days and nights essentially in the provinces of his mind looking for the capital. He entered the university and took a degree in law and another in literature. He also qualified by competitive examination for an unsalaried library position, and then never started work. For several years his best efforts went into two complementary activities: writing short stories and literary sketches for the newspapers and symbolist reviews, and cultivating the elegant families of the friends he had made at school and during military service. He memorialized his success in both lines with the publication of his first collection, *Pleasures and Days* (1896). It was an overly elegant edition illustrated by a salon hostess, Madeleine Lemaire, with a preface extorted from Anatole France. It looked like the work of a dilettante with powerful connections, even though it does not read that way.

The strongest presence in Proust's life at this juncture was Comte Robert de Montesquiou-Fezensac. Fifteen years older, he had everything Proust thought he wanted. The Count was descended from the model for D'Artagnan of *The Three Musketeers* and could claim most of European nobility as relatives by blood or marriage. Immense wealth enabled him to cultivate an esthetic manner and way of life remarkable enough to have already inspired one notorious book, Huysmans' *A rebours*. He was also a published poet of some note and flaunted his homosexuality with enormous style. Proust fawned on him for several years before he could pull away, and the fascination never disappeared entirely. When Montesquiou mentioned his young friend once in print, Proust had to fight a pistol duel with a critic who seized the occasion to ridicule him as "one of those small-time fops in literary heat." No one was hurt.

The Dreyfus Affair exploded in November 1897. Proust, aged twenty-six, was intensely committed to the Dreyfus cause from the start. He helped get Anatole

France's signature for the Petition of the Intellectuals, attended every session of Zola's trial, and was active in support of Colonel Picquart, the second hero of the affair. This public behavior placed Proust in the opposite camp from both his family (his father knew practically every minister) and most of his society hostesses. He recorded the harrowing tension and the human consequences of these events in sections of a novel he had been working on in spurts and fragments for some four years. *Jean Santeuil* provides scenes from the sad yet charmed life of a young man who can never pull himself together and is forever protected from above. After some eight-hundred pages without form or continuity, Proust abandoned the manuscript in apparent dissatisfaction.

He was still in the provinces. His next discovery was John Ruskin, the English art critic and social thinker. Between 1899 and 1905 Proust spent much of his time reading him and making "pilgrimages" to the sites in France and Italy about which Ruskin had written. He went on to translate two of Ruskin's books (with the help of his mother and an English girl friend), and to write prefaces that grew until they almost swallowed the texts they were intended to present. Proust performed a dance with Ruskin similar to the one he had performed with Montesquiou. For a time Ruskin's combination of esthetic sensitivity, scholarship, and social thought won his deep admiration. Later he found Ruskin guilty of a false idolatry of art and of a masked moralism. This long encounter with Ruskin was deeply profitable for Proust. He was able to clarify his own ideas on art and to acknowledge to himself that fiction was still his goal. In 1902, at the peak of his Ruskin absorption, he wrote to Prince Antoine Bibesco:

> . . . a hundred characters for novels, a thousand ideas keep asking me to give them substance, like those shades that keep asking Ulysses in the *Odyssey* to give

them blood to drink and bring them to life, and that the hero pushes aside with his sword.

At thirty, Proust was already a deeply eccentric man, and still living at home on an allowance. His preferred schedule of rising in the late afternoon and going to bed at dawn estranged him from his own family. The events of the next few years came perilously close to paralyzing him. His younger brother, a doctor following in their father's footsteps, married in 1903 and set up on his own. At the wedding Marcel was a grotesque, semi-invalid figure in several overcoats and mufflers. A few months later their father died, and Mme Proust devoted herself for two years to caring for Proust's asthma and hay fever, and helping him translate Ruskin. She also organized dinners for his friends in their apartment. Then, after a short illness, Mme Proust died in 1905. Her son lay for almost two months in sleepless seclusion in the apartment, and then spent six weeks in a private clinic. After this, his nocturnal and neurotic behavior became more pronounced than ever.

The shift I have mentioned in Proust's career took place over the next four years—not a single event or development, but a gradual convergence of forces already at work. He began to withdraw slowly from his salon life and saw his friends in restaurants late at night. He could now have homosexual affairs by hiring young men as chauffeurs or secretaries. Writing a series of literary pastiches increased his conviction that he must find his own style and his own form. Meanwhile, his writing was becoming more and more autobiographical. In 1908 his drafts of a projected critical essay, *Against Sainte-Beuve*, kept turning into personal narrative whenever he let them take their course. If Proust had any revelation, it must have been the discovery that he could accommodate his irresistible autobiographical impulse in the novel form. During a lull in his writing in January 1909, he apparently had an unexpected and compelling surge of memory over a cup of tea into which he dipped some dry toast. When he described the incident in the preface he was writing for *Against Sainte-Beuve*, a number of similar reminiscences came to mind. Some missing element had fallen into place, and now it seemed as if he were at work on a wholly new book. Yet it was really the same one—the book begun in *Pleasures and Days*, tried again and laid aside in *Jean Santeuil*, tried once more in the anecdotal pages that open the preface to Ruskin's *Sesame and Lilies*, carried on in *Against Sainte-Beuve*. Endowed with a new plan but no firm title, this transmuted work took possession of him during the spring of 1909 and filled the rest of his life. By August, he wrote proudly and optimistically to Mme Emile Strauss, one of his hostesses: "I have begun—and finished—a whole long book." About the same time he gave a few details to Alfred Vallette, a possible publisher for it.

> I'm finishing a book which, in spite of its provisional title, *Against Sainte-Beuve: Recollection of a Morning*, is a genuine novel and an indecent novel in some of its sections. The book ends with a long conversation on Sainte-Beuve and aesthetics.

We should probably be grateful that Vallette refused Proust's novel then, for it was many years and hundreds of pages away from being finished. But at least it was begun, and already getting out of control.

These developments were the signal for Proust to modify his life of indecision and distraction. In the fall of 1909 he announced to his friends a kind of withdrawal and retreat, referring mysteriously yet resolutely to the long work ahead of him. His caginess about the title and plan of his novel made it sound like a scientific discovery or a military secret. In 1910 he sealed himself into the bedroom of his new apartment by lining it with cork, and sent out irregular reports on the page count he had reached. A few close friends like Georges de Lauris and Reynaldo Hahn, sworn to confidence, were allowed to read the oilcloth covered notebooks. They gave him the encouragement he needed. Of course, Proust did not retire completely from Parisian life as he had known it. He kept up with his friends and, at intervals, muffled in outlandish clothes, dropped in on an elegant hostess just as her party was breaking up. He even went occasionally to a music hall or an art gallery, and he listened to concerts and plays by subscribing to a service that allowed members to hear live performances over the telephone. But from now until his death in 1922, his novel took precedence over everything else. The tide had turned. His forays into the outer world and the bulk of his letters were either means of obtaining information for his writings or attempts to arrange the proper publication and reception for his work. For the latter purpose he pulled every string, used every connection, and called in every outstanding debt available to him. Yet four publishing houses refused his book. After a cursory look, André Gide turned it down for Gallimard as too snobbish and amateurish. He soon changed his mind. Grasset, a new house, finally published it, at the author's expense, in 1913. All Proust's advance work was barely sufficient to launch this first of two projected volumes. By the time Gallimard published the second volume after the war, the manuscript had grown unsuppressibly, frighteningly, like a carnivorous vine that would finally entwine and devour its owner.

The remainder of Proust's life takes on a mythological quality. His nocturnal, bedridden, disorderly work habits seem heroic. In his private life he mixed low-grade hedonism with deliberate psychological and moral experiment. What looks degraded to some of us may be edifying to others. This man of shrewd medical insight mercilessly punished his frail body and refused proper advice, even from his brother. He followed what he told Louis de Robert was his "only rule": "to yield to one's demon, to one's thought, to write on everything to the

point of exhaustion." When he was awarded the prestigious Goncourt prize in 1919 for the second volume
of the novel, *A l'ombre des jeunes filles en fleurs*, the
event barely ruffled the waters in his special universe of
nurture and devotion. His work had become a living
being, making demands of its own. "For me it had turned
into a son. The dying mother must still submit to the
fatigue of taking care of him" (III, 1941–42). He knew
he had given birth.

The last decade of Proust's life displays an outward
life gradually abdicated in favor of a work—both the
inward process and the material product. Yet there is
nothing reluctant or tragic about his abdication. It does
not resemble the two great royal departures of the era,
when a Spanish king bowed to republicanism and an
English king chose love of a commoner over royalty.
With surprising confidence Proust simply decided in
favor of the dense tropical growth he felt within him.
For he discovered that it was at last assuming a shape
it had not exhibited earlier. Throughout his life, Proust
composed in a discontinuous fashion. Except possibly
in the earliest short stories, he did not start at the beginning of a narrative and follow it through to the end.
Observations and incidents and characters came to him
in disparate fragments directly based on his day-to-day
experience. His notebooks seem to be in total disarray
in spite of the dazzling insights they carry. In reading
Jean Santeuil, still virtually a notebook, one rarely receives the sense of a direction in which events are
moving. It drifts to a standstill. The prose pieces Proust
wrote for the abandoned essay-novel, *Against Sainte-
Beuve*, display this desultory quality to an even greater
extent. He seems totally at sea.

But after 1909 he has a chart and a course. The "very
exacting composition" Proust lays claim to in a letter
to Louis de Robert in 1912 was the major new element
that had entered his work and claimed his energies. In
the *Search* he holds his characters and his story in an

iron grasp. Lengthy digressions and hernia-like extensions of a single scene or sentiment do not mean that
he has lost track of where his characters are going and
what they have already been through. Considering its
length, unfinished condition, and the handicapped circumstances in which he wrote the novel, it contains
extraordinarily few repetitions and inconsistencies. The
over-all design and the narrative links rarely waver, a
difficult feat in view of the complex strategies of divul-
gence and development he set for himself. Yet Proust
never relished the final stage of assembling and fitting.
"Writing is easy for me," he wrote Gallimard. "But to
patch things together, to set all the bones, that's more
than I can face. For some time I've realized that I leave
out the best pieces, because I would have to fit this
detail to that one, and so on." Even so, beneath all that
flesh Proust did set the bones of his narrative and created strong joints to carry the sustained movements of
its development.

The other major shift in Proust's writing after 1909
concerns the narrative voice in which he wrote. With a
few revealing exceptions, *Jean Santeuil* employs the
third person to designate a "hero" very close to Proust
in biographical and psychological terms. The opening
pages of *On Reading*, and the preface to *Against Sainte-
Beuve* use the *I* without feint or dissembling to represent
Proust as a real person and signatory. In none of these
texts has he found his true discursive pitch and pace.
Somewhere in the early stages of the *Search*, however,
when he still thought it was *Against Sainte-Beuve*, a
double reaction occurs. It is both a fusion and a fission
attacking the *I*. First of all Proust calls in both the
scantily veiled third-person of *Jean Santeuil* and his
various uses of the first person. He combines them into
the *je* of the *Search*—both narrator and character, a
double personage in one pronoun. At the same time
Proust takes himself, his life, and his character, and
divides them up among a number of characters in the

novel: Charlus, Bloch, Swann, as well as Marcel and the Narrator.

This fission-fusion process explains why it is so unsatisfactory to keep asking if Marcel or the Narrator represents Proust. There can be no doubt that the *Search* embodies a version—both revelation and disguise—of Proust's life. The links are too evident to discount, from the setting and action to details like the Narrator having translated Ruskin's *Sesame and Lilies*. But Proust's disclaimers are equally powerful. He insists that his book be read as a self-contained story and not as autobiography masquerading as fiction. It would be foolish to insist on one of these approaches to the exclusion of the other. Toward the end of the novel one comes upon an odd passage which makes a tiny step toward reconciliation. There is nothing like it elsewhere in the *Search*.

> In this book, in which every fact is fictional and in which not a single character is based on a living person, in which everything has been invented by me according to the needs of my demonstration, I must state to the credit of my country that only Françoise's millionaire relatives, who interrupted their retirement in order to help their needy niece, are real people, existing in the world (III, 846).

Here, I believe, Proust is pointing out to us a kind of vestigial navel cord, a detail which proves that his vast work does not coincide with actuality but was born from it. Ideas of slow gestation and final parturition do greater justice to the novel's origins than concepts of literal imitation or of complete autonomy.

In Proust's final years the autobiographical nature of the *Search* seems less significant than the literary nature of its author's life. He prepares us for this perspective with the much quoted line in which he attacks the failure of Sainte-Beuve's critical method to take into account what true wisdom should have told him: ". . . that a book is the product of a different self from the

one we display in our habits, in society, in our vices"
(*CSB*, 221–22). This may be as close as we can come
to gospel. But there is a further question. Need we
assume that the authorial self has been formed prior
to the composition of the work? Valéry liked to point
out that, as the criminal may be the product of
his crime, so the author may be the product of his
literary work. What I have said about Proust's "abdication" points to a sense in which, *as author*, he was the
product of his work in progress. In the cases most crucial
to literature, writing is less a record of what has actually
happened to someone than a discovery-creation of what
might potentially happen to people, "author" included.
The symbiotic relationship between man and book grows
as much out of aesthetic as out of biographical factors.
The development of "the other self" who wrote the
Search can be traced within the novel itself, but not in
terms of finding keys to characters and identifying incidents transposed from Proust's life. They are incidentals.
Mysteriously and steadily, the *Search* secreted its true
author, the literary creature we call Marcel Proust.

The biographical Proust spent his last three years in
bed, in great part in order to escape the demands of
literary celebrity. Surrounded by galley proofs, manuscripts, and strange potions, he lived his unfinished book
as totally and exclusively as an author can without
losing his sense of reality. What kept him sane and
even practical was the desire to assure his work an
enlightened readership. He answered most letters (but
not one from an American girl who had read his novel
steadily for three years and then rebuked him: "Don't
be a *poseur*. . . . Tell me in two lines what you wished
to say"), contributed to newspaper surveys on trends
and styles, and took time to write two superb essays on
his masters: Flaubert and Baudelaire. His remarks about
the tonality of tenses and the place of metaphor in their
work apply also to his own. An occasional Lazarus-like
sortie formed part of the pattern. Shot up with adren-

alin and caffeine, he submitted to a ceremonial mid-
night meeting with James Joyce at a large supper party
for Diaghilev, Picasso, and Stravinsky. Neither author
had read the other's work. They talked about the only
other subject that mattered to them: their health. Another time, Proust let himself be taken to the fashionable
1920s nightspot, le Boeuf sur le toît. He never shed his
heavy overcoat and was almost swept into a drunken
brawl. Meanwhile the work never stopped, even during
the final months. Most of all Proust feared the affliction
that had tortured Baudelaire at the end: aphasia. Yet,
beneath the complaints, Proust found a wonderful excitement in the tension between his mission to finish
his work and his simple mortality. Three months before
the end, he answered "a little question" submitted to
various prominent persons by the newspaper, *l'Intransi-
geant*: "If the world were coming to an end, what would
it mean to you?"

> I believe that life would suddenly appear wonderful
> to us, if we were suddenly threatened with death as
> you propose.

Death had long since become his faith, his inspiration.
The final complication was pneumonia. He died on
November 18, 1922.

AN OVERDETERMINED UNIVERSE

At intervals throughout the *Search*, Marcel goes to
stay in a strange place. Each time it is as if he has to
reconstitute from scratch all his perceptions and habits,
the whole orientation of his life. Toward the middle of
the novel, he visits his close friend Saint-Loup in Doncières, a town where Saint-Loup is doing his military
service in the cavalry. What strikes Marcel first on
arriving is the "perpetual, musical, and warlike vibra-
tility" (II, 70) that hangs in the air. For several pages
after that the whole narrative texture is woven out of

unfamiliar sounds. He notices Saint-Loup's modified accent. The crackling fire in his friend's barracks room makes Marcel think that someone must be in there while he stands listening in the hall outside the closed door. Once he enters the empty room, the ticking of an unseen clock seems to come from all directions until Marcel has spotted it and given the object and the sound a specific location. And then this acoustical disorientation infects everything, even Marcel's friendship for Saint-Loup and his sense of his own identity in the world. In other words, when his impressions are most vivid, he loses his bearings. Marcel's "auditory hyperesthesia" (II, 72), which Saint-Loup specifically mentions here as making life difficult for his visitor, serves not to fix the world more clearly in place for Marcel but to send it skittering off toward new patterns and multiple vanishing points. The disconcerting effect of strange sounds throws every element of life into play again, and thus into jeopardy. Even familiar sensations recover significance and urgency.

This dense network of perpetually reconstituted connections between impressions, feelings, meanings, and words constitutes one of the fundamental qualities of Proust's work. He conveys it in the resonance of the prose and in the over-all architecture of the action. The superb opening "scene," in which the Narrator puts himself together like Humpty-Dumpty out of fragmentary impressions of waking and dreaming, is baffling at first. Nothing created out of so many elements could be simple. Even when the Narrator fails to achieve this self-creation *ex omnibus* (dialectically the equivalent of *ex nihilo*), the writing itself emits a powerful sense of the links among the things around us and our experiences of them. Proust writes from deep inside the world of Baudelaire's *correspondances*, close to Leonardo's universe where the painter said he saw actual lines connecting objects in a kind of visible geometry.

In one respect this sense of the plenitude of relations

between things runs counter to a human temper often treated in modern literature. In writers like Kafka and Camus we discern a quality of emptiness which it is hard to describe. For K and Meursault, experience generates very little motivation to undertake anything, to oppose the world or to affirm oneself. They act out of gratuitous impulse or yield to mere circumstance. In Proust the opposite is true. Multiple desires and motivations converge on every action and often impede its execution. Marcel goes to unbelievable lengths to explain to himself the behavior of the women in his life. For them as for him potential motives are often spelled out in a series of either/or propositions. But one motive will never prove to be the correct one and eliminate the others. After two pages of speculation on the character and behavior of one of his oldest friends, Gilberte Swann, Marcel throws up his hands. "None of these hypotheses was absurd" (III, 708). The mystery of Proust's world arises not from gratuitousness or from the absence of motivation but from the conflictingly overdetermined quality of most actions, and from the adaptability of most actions to a great number of attributions. Until Marcel reaches a wider wisdom, what happens around him is not indifferent but overwhelming.

How to Read a Roman-fleuve[1]

PRACTICAL MATTERS

Prospective Proust readers have to make a series of decisions that can be best expressed as questions with tentative answers.

In what language should one read Proust? Anyone who can comfortably read Balzac or Tocqueville or Camus in the original should tackle the *Search* in French. The translation will not turn out to be much easier for him, and he should at least make the attempt. Because of the résumés and indices it contains, the three-volume Pléiade edition in French has great advantages over the inexpensive seven-volume pocket edition. To the reader restricted to English, I can

[1] This chapter is addressed to those seeking guidance for a first reading of Proust. Readers already familiar with the *Search* and looking for commentary on its shape and significance should skip to Chapter III.

state that the Moncrieff translation is a sustained piece of craftsmanship with a recognizable style in English that echoes the original. But Moncrieff is not infallible. Occasionally he Bowdlerizes. It is hard to excuse some of his clumsy errors.[2]

Unfortunately, Moncrieff died before reaching the seventh and last volume. The recent translation of it by Andreas Mayor represents both a continuity with Moncrieff's style and a sensible approach to problems of transposition from a very ragged original text. Considering the immense labor of translating Proust, we are well served in English.[3]

A reader whose French is shaky should probably work with Moncrieff. Yet I know several enterprising individuals who have laid out the French and English texts

[2] One example should suffice. Moncrieff's confusion over pronouns shifts the hesitations of Swann's sensibility into Odette's mind. Nothing could be more out of character.

Et ce fut Swann qui, avant qu'elle laissât tomber [son visage], comme malgré elle, sur ses lèvres, le retint un instant, à quelque distance, entre ses deux mains. Il avait voulu laisser à sa pensée le temps d'accourir, de reconnaître le rêve qu'elle avait si longtemps caressé et d'assister à sa réalisation, comme une parente qu'on appelle pour prendre sa part du succès d'un enfant qu'elle a beaucoup aimé (I, 233).

And Swann it was who, before she allowed her face, as though despite her efforts, to fall upon his lips, held it back for a moment longer, at a little distance between his hands. He had intended to leave time for her mind to overtake her body's movements, to recognize the dream which she had so long cherished and to assist at its realisation, like a mother invited as a spectator when a prize is given to the child she has reared and loved. (Moncrieff's translation.)

With the minimum of correction, the second sentence should read: "He had intended to leave time for his mind to overtake his body's movements, to recognize the dream which it had so long cherished. . . ." In the next sentence, *parente* means "relative."

[3] The *Search* has also been translated in full into fifteen other languages.

side by side and developed their own gymnastic method for straddling these two platforms.

In either language one has to read with a kind of patient faith that Proust is not leading us down the garden path and that he will bring the sentence, the scene, and the book to a clear conclusion. And so he does. He tells us himself that he is forever tacking against the wind, and describes a mind "following its habitual course, which moves foward by digressions, going off obliquely in one direction and then in the other" (II, 816). In order to follow this course of advance by indirection, I believe it is best to approach the reading of Proust as if it were a kind of long-term cure, or an initiation to unfamiliar mental and physical movements evolved by another culture. A steady, leisurely pace, without the tension of fixed deadlines, serves best. Certain habits of thought can thus be laid aside as others are slowly acquired. It may take months, even years. The *Search* creates a season of the mind outside temporal limits.

How many of the 3000 *pages should one read?* How much food or drink is enough? The reader should probably not decide the question in advance and should let his appetite guide him. Some will stop short, scoffing, in the opening pages. Others will continue in absorption to the last page and then start over again. Many more will ask for a middle way, and they should be shown one. We have Frazer and Gibbon in one-volume editions. With great profit as a boy I read *Don Quijote* and *Robinson Crusoe*, *Arabian Nights*, and *Gulliver's Travels* in truncated children's editions. When copyright expires, will we be offered a pocket Proust? In *Search of Lost Time* in three-hundred pages? The prospect is not utterly unthinkable. As in the classics mentioned above, there is in Proust a deep universal element, an esthetic consciousness, that may one day reach many more people than can read his novel. A film might open the way, though it seems unlikely. Several ambitious projects have already collapsed. Another by Losey and Pinter is under way. A Frenchman wrote a novel a few years ago which describes at length the effect of a reading of Proust's novel on his central character. Yet such surrogates seem inadequate. Even a sensitive anthology of set pieces and self-contained reflections cannot represent Proust, for it conveys no sense of the whole or of the underlying movement. The resourceful independent reader will thread his own way through the text and take sensible short cuts. On the other hand, reading Proust in an organized course with a competent teacher to set the level of understanding and interpretation and with perceptive students willing to participate in class discussions can develop into a very rewarding collective experience. But a term or semester course is too short and often leads to intense frustration at the end.

Though few have ever been proposed in print, there are various ways of reading approximately a third of the *Search* and supplying the missing sections through summaries.[4] Proust's other writings, though they have various merits, can wait until one has fully assimilated the *Search*.

Are there devices or approaches that can facilitate one's reading? Both in translation and in the original, Proust slows most readers down. His sentences move through long spirals that will not be hastened. He offers few paragraph breaks to declare the steps and stages of his thought. Unlike most nineteenth-century novelists

[4] The following is one suggestion, which any Proustian could criticize: *Swann's Way* (the first three quarters: "Combray" and "Swann in Love"); *Within a Budding Grove* (Part Two: "Balbec"); *Guermantes's Way* (II, Chapter One: "The Grandmother's Death"); *Sodom and Gomorrah* (first thirty pages and the last thirty: "Charlus and Albertine"); *The Captive* (first thirty pages and two hundred pages on the concert at the Verdurins arranged by Charlus); *The Sweet Cheat Gone* (omit); *Time Regained* (first thirty pages and the last two hundred: "Combray" again, and the last reception and reflections on writing). . . .

he does not construct out of short chapters that divide the story into convenient mental mouthfuls. One simply cannot force one's speed and hope to register the prose. Gradually, however, it can come to sound appropriate and effective.

When you look at it closely, no passage in Proust seems typical. The patterns he makes are numerous and contrasting. But it may be helpful to consider one medium-long sentence in order to pick out a few stylistic features that are recognizably his. The sentence quoted below appears in an important juncture at the beginning of *Swann's Way*. Swann is an elegant, wealthy Jew, much sought after in the best Parisian · society. His worldly milieu has made him both sensitive and blasé. He devotes most of his life to a series of love affairs with women from all classes who happen to catch his eye. His story begins against this background.

> But, *whereas* each of these liaisons, or each of these flirtations, had been the more or less complete realization of a dream inspired by the sight of a face or body that Swann had, spontaneously, without effort, found attractive, on the contrary, *when* one day at the theater he was introduced to Odette de Crécy by one of his former friends, who spoke of her as a charming woman with whom he might get along, but painted her as more difficult than she really was in order to seem to have done him a bigger favor in introducing him, *she appeared to Swann not unattractive certainly but to have a kind of beauty that was indifferent to him*, that did not stir his desire, even inspired a kind of physical repulsion in him, to be the sort of woman, as happens to all of us in different ways, who is the opposite of what our senses ask for (I, 195–96) [Italics added].

By linking more than a dozen subordinate clauses to the ends of one principal clause, Proust has composed a difficult sentence. But the fully articulated syntax and the rhythm it enforces firmly direct the reading. The emphatic initial *But*, commands attention. Immediately following, *whereas* projects far out ahead an organizing power that lasts until it is picked up by *when* and carried on to the central statement. The construction here is more sturdy than subtle. Why does Proust write one sentence instead of three or four? What is the effect?

Had he used several sentences, he would have had to rely on modifiers and rhetorical devices to bring out the central proposition. Or he would have had to delete details. In the sentence as written, subordination serves to arrange a large amount of material around the clause: "she appeared . . . indifferent to him. . . ." The facts that the introduction took place in the theater, and that she was not presented as a woman of easy virtue, are minor yet revealing details. Proust uses the nuances and hierarchies of syntax to hold these details in perspective. Furthermore, the very relationships expressed by the connectives (*whereas, when, who*; in other contexts he concentrates on causative, concessive, or conditional relations) form an essential part of Proust's subject. This sentence contrives to tell us not only the circumstances under which Swann first met Odette but also to suggest the whole sinuous course of their love affair. Before that interlude his life followed a recognizable pattern; during it that pattern is so disrupted as to leave a deep mark on Swann; and at its close (I, 382) he looks back at its surprising beginning (and in effect at this very sentence) to wonder bemusedly how it ever happened. A great number of complex, half-understood circumstances converge on any significant event, and then diverge toward a future of undivulged possibilities. The passage just quoted is one example of how Proust's prose tends to reproduce that plenitude. He wants to make us see that intersection of lines. Compare the similar yet distinctly more serpentine movement of the sentence that begins, "Then, like a city . . .," in the document reproduced in the Appendix (page 170). One could, of course, go much further. Mallarmé wrote his most ambitious poem "Un coup de dés" in the form of a single, repeatedly proliferating, meticulously articulated sentence. If a novelist begins to experience both time and meaning as fundamentally continuous, he might well aspire to write one unbroken sentence, paralleling consciousness itself, shadowing or even overshadowing reality. Though tempted by such a course, Proust pulled back before he abandoned syntax and readability. He shaped the world of his fiction by forming it into high relief in his prose, not by flattening it out endlessly or by cutting it up into little pieces. This same principle of fullness explains his effective use, at long intervals, of a contrasting device: the tersest possible form of declaration, a staccato phrase, an abrupt question. "It was himself." "Dead forever?" "My whole being capsized." The flowing periods of his prose create extended stretches of lived time. They also set the scene for unexpected and devastating reversals which occur in very few words. We notice the lengthiness more than the brevity, and, indeed, there is more of the former. Both belong to the fullness of his style.

The best way to discover and respond to Proust's expressive voice, as well as the deliberate pacing of his narrative, is to hear the prose, to read it aloud. For he often works by a kind of mimicry at one remove, echoing and aping his characters without abandoning the steady flow of his own thought. The unnamed Norwegian philosopher speaks a totally different French from that of Dr. Cottard or of Odette, and we are allowed to hear each of them. Without an auditory sense of the text, even in its most reflective and interior passages, the visual field of urelieved print tends to become oppressive. Translations cannot convey the original texture, yet on this score Moncrieff performs remarkably well. He will bear reading aloud.

Apart from the speech rhythm and inflections stirred up by the text, there are two other items a reader can watch for to help him find his way. Proust frequently

employs a recurrent narrative detail or incident as a
kind of refrain to orient the course of action. In the
"Combray" section, fifty pages of pure description are
pinned together by the minute mystery of whether or
not Mme Goupil got to mass on time. For Swann, the
question of who was with Odette the afternoon she did
not answer her doorbell becomes the very axis of his
life. Marcel develops an imaginary passion for Baronne
de Putbus's reputedly sexy maid, whom he has never
laid eyes on. He keeps trying to trace her, always without
success, in a series of maneuvers that span the latter
half of the novel. These colored strands surface just
often enough in the narrative fabric to help reveal its
pattern.

The other feature a reader would do well to remain
on the alert for carries more significance than the narrative refrains. It reveals the plastic quality of the
action. From time to time in the story Marcel is told or
discovers a small item of information which, when fully
grasped and fitted into place, changes his entire perspective on the relationship between important characters or
on the nature of human conduct. The aging down-to-
earth Marquise de Villeparisis, a girlhood friend of
Marcel's grandmother, turns out to be closely related
to the aristocratic and inaccessible Guermantes, whom
he intensely desires to know. The eminent painter, Elstir,
turns out to be the same person as Biche, or Tiche, the
ridiculous and vulgar young man in Mme Verdurin's
first "little clan." The battle of Méséglise in World War I
makes that village famous in world history; yet the
Combray church, the incarnation of Marcel's childhood
and of French history, is destroyed. A hint is passed in
the closing pages that the virtuous Duchesse de Guermantes may not, after all, have always been the most
faithful of wives. These tiny shocks profoundly modify
the great web of relations and reactions that constitute
the substance of the book. One must read Proust as
carefully as a detective story in which any detail may

become a clue to everything else. Every page tends toward the accumulation of the familiar, the security of habit, in order to establish the sense of location and identity we all need. At the same time every page glows with a blend of excitement and anxiety over the possible introduction of a new element. We half anticipate a break in routine which will disrupt the pattern and launch the whole setting into unpredictable motion. This ambivalent mood, which seems to posit boredom as the inevitable background for excitement, emerges beautifully in "Combray." The *train-train* or unvarying daily round of events that characterizes life in Aunt Léonie's house is both tested and reinforced by the "asymetrical Saturday" (I, 110). On that day each week lunch is served a full hour early to allow Françoise to go to market. The variation, astonishing to everyone, is itself assimilated into the routine. Yet the risk of that established departure from schedule prepares the way for all the dismay and despair to come when this tight little life falls apart.

THE ELEMENTS OF THE STORY

The biggest help in reading Proust is to have the persons and places of the story clear in one's mind. For this purpose I have arranged the elements in tables and diagrams to accompany the prose exposition that follows.

The *Search* has five major settings (see Diagram I). I mention places before persons because so much of the action consists of Marcel's gradual and painful accommodation to new settings, and of the association of character with particularities of place. Albertine *is* essentially Balbec incarnate and carries always within her the sensuousness of flowers and the mutability of the sea. Furthermore, all geography in Proust, from ocean to bed to church steeple, is symbolic, even animistic. "The various places of the earth are also beings, whose per-

I. PLACES

Combray	Paris	Balbec	Doncières	Venice
Church of St.-Hilaire	Champs-Elysées Gardens	Grand Hôtel	Cavalry Barracks	(Trip planned and canceled)
Aunt Léonie's House	Guermantes's Town House	Beach	Hotel de Flandre	Visit with Mother
Swann's Way (Méséglise) (Tansonville)	Marcel's Family's Apartment	Elstir's Studio	Pension	
Guermantes's Way	Salons	Rivebelle		
Martinville Steeples	Houses of Prostitution	La Raspelière		

sonality is so strong that some people die of being separated from them" (*JS*, 96, 534).

The first setting is the village of COMBRAY, presumably near Chartres. (Proust later shifts it eastward into the World War I combat zone.) Marcel and his parents spend vacations there. Aunt Léonie's house and the village church are described as if one would never seek to appeal from their simple reality to a higher realm. Combray embodies the solidarity of family origins as well as the roots of French civilization—Church, people, royalty. The two "ways" along which Marcel and his family take their walks divide the countryside, and the universe, into two irreconcilable and seemingly inaccessible worlds. Marcel will eventually penetrate into both: the Guermantes's way, or the aristocracy with all its remote mysteries; and Swann's way, a worldly, artistic domain tinged with evil and scandal. After the opening two-hundred pages, Combray does not again become the setting of the story except for a brief section in the last volume. Yet it is never out of mind.

PARIS, where most of the novel takes place, is reduced to a few elements. At first everything revolves around the Champs-Elysées gardens where Marcel meets Gilberte Swann as a playmate. Later Marcel and his family move to a new apartment attached to the town house of the Duc and Duchesse de Guermantes. Around this complex of rooms, courtyards, and shops, the streets lead away to two further regions: the various salons to which Marcel is invited, and the houses of ill repute he later stumbles into or visits.

BALBEC is an imaginary seaside resort town in Normandy or Brittany, closely modeled on Cabourg, whose beaches attracted great numbers of French and English summer visitors at the turn of the century. (The Grand Hôtel still stands next to the beach in Cabourg, a massive building with long corridors and a slow-moving, open-cage elevator.) Marcel drives occasionally to Rivebelle, where there is a good restaurant. Elstir's studio is

on the beach at Balbec. It is out of this very seascape
that "the young girls in bloom" seem to materialize;
they arouse Marcel's most enduring desires. A short
train ride along the coast brings one to La Raspelière,
the estate rented during the summer by the Verdurins.

Inland from Balbec lies the military town of DON-
CIÈRES, where Saint-Loup is doing his service in the
cavalry. Marcel here makes his first long stay away
from his family. On returning to Paris he suddenly perceives his grandmother as a complete stranger, an old
lady approaching death.

Early in the novel Marcel's father decides that the
family will make a trip to VENICE. Marcel becomes so
overwrought with anticipation that the trip has to be
canceled. The image of Venice haunts him all his life
until he finally makes the journey with his mother long
after the desire to do so has passed.

Through these five settings several hundred named
characters circulate. Most of them are minor, and their
number includes many historical figures who flit by,
barely glimpsed on the outer edges of the events. About
twenty-five characters carry the central action (see
Diagram II).

From start to finish there is someone in the novel
saying I. Like the single Martinville spire on the horizon,
which separates into two and then three steeples as one
approaches it, different voices and different beings step
out from behind that first-person singular. Yet the lin-
guistic and semidramatic illusion of their unity inside
a single pronoun is one of the principal devices used in
the book to weld together the disparate levels of identity
and narrative, and to permit rapid shifts among different
modes of discourse. The I in Proust is an eternal pivot
chord. Marcel Muller, the most careful analyst of this
aspect of Proust's work, distinguishes seven distinct I's.
Let us here be content with two, plus a self-effacing
third.

II. CHARACTERS

I	Family	Early Friends	Guermantes	Artists	Others
Marcel	Mother	Françoise	Marquise de Villeparisis	Bergotte	M. and Mme Verdurin
Narrator	Grandmother	Swann	Saint-Loup	Elstir	Albertine
(Author)	Aunt Léonie	Odette	Charlus	Vinteuil	Cottard
	Father	Gilberte	Duc and Duchesse	La Berma	Jupien
	Uncle Adolphe	Bloch	Prince and Princesse	Rachel	Norpois
		Legrandin	Mlle de Saint-Loup	Morel	

MARCEL, the boy who grows up in the course of the novel and who does not know at any given point what the future holds for him, says *I*. Though the given name, "Marcel" (with no family name to complete it), is mentioned only twice in 3000 pages—and even then skittishly and not for direct attribution—I feel that no other designation will serve for the "hero" as he develops in the narrative. Secondly, the NARRATOR says *I*; he is Marcel grown old and become a writer who, as he tells his own story in roughly chronological order, both reflects on it and refers to events that violate the chronology. Thirdly, on the rare occasions when he materializes beside the two others, the AUTHOR says *I*. He is not the biographical Proust but his literary persona, commenting on his novel and its relation to truth and reality. Within and around the essentially double *I* of the story sparks a constant arc of irony, sympathy, and regret. Marcel and the Narrator move slowly toward one another across the long reaches of the book, constantly signaling, sometimes lost, until they finally meet in the closing pages. That reunited *I*, like Plato's lovers, produces a whole which is the book itself.

Along the way, this linguistically single yet ontologically double *I* produces several curious effects. In spite of his constant efforts to do so, Marcel never adequately beholds himself and cannot really believe in his identity or his role. As a result, it is as if a segment of negative space occupies the center of the action, a hole in the fabric. Marcel eludes himself and eludes us. We never learn what he really looks like. He seems as much of an absence as a presence. Understandably, the reader has difficulty identifying with this inchoate creature and spends a portion of his time sifting the evidence and supplying appearances and character traits to square with the reported events. The Narrator collaborates by presenting Marcel as piteous, weak-willed, egotistical, and sometimes downright deceitful. Yet somehow Marcel makes his way in the world and seems to have more friends than enemies. This wayward and uncertain nature of the principal character gives the reader an active part to play. He cannot coast through the incidents by stepping into the shoes of the hero. Identification does not function. The reader must seek out the Marcel almost crouching behind the events and reluctant to be brought forward as a person with a name and a recognizable character.

These fluctuations in the first person of Proust's novel also mean that the question of omniscience is never settled. There are only conflicting claims. Marcel observes everything yet cannot trust his perceptions. What he learns from experience is that appearances deceive us. The Narrator commands wide knowledge and often speaks with a wisdom that seems to rise above the transitory. For he has learned that general laws and character types inlay our experience with many striking regularities. The shadowy figure of the Author lurks behind them both, barely whispering that knowledge comes of having truly lived one's life and belongs therefore to death. These approaches to wisdom vie with one another throughout the *Search*. The simplest aspect of the novel, the presence of an *I* speaking, leads into unforeseen complexities and subtleties held together primarily by that speaking *I*. In the pages that follow I shall try to distinguish carefully between "Marcel" and "the Narrator," but that terminology will not do full justice to their counterpoint in the text.

In the course of his life Marcel moves among several recognizable groups of characters. The members of his family form the most compact group. In fact his MOTHER and GRANDMOTHER virtually fuse into a single maternal presence that hovers over Marcel until close to the end. AUNT LÉONIE is an eccentric imaginary-invalid, who keeps track of every living thing in Combray from her top-floor observation post. As he ages, Marcel comes to resemble her in many respects. The FATHER's undefined professional eminence and official connections inspire awe and respect. UNCLE ADOLPHE, the black sheep of the family who keeps mistresses and lives high, leaves an indelible impression on Marcel.

Second, there are the various people Marcel knows from his childhood in Combray and who for that reason alone form a class apart. FRANÇOISE, the eternal and ever-present servant, embodies the durability of the peasantry and the stern demands of a muse. SWANN, a wealthy Jewish neighbor with unassuming manners and an entree to the most elegant Parisian society, is the first person to trouble Marcel's secure world. Swann's earlier love affair and eventual marriage with the cocotte ODETTE sets the motifs of Marcel's own career. Their daughter, GILBERTE, is his first love. LEGRANDIN, the local snob, and BLOCH, a precocious ill-mannered comrade, also enter the story in Combray. The Swann family preoccupies Marcel until he becomes obsessed by the noble family of Guermantes.

Long after the apparition of the DUCHESSE DE GUERMANTES in the Combray church, Marcel meets the members of this group in strict order of ascending social rank: The MARQUISE DE VILLEPARISIS, a school friend of Marcel's grandmother; her nephew, the MARQUIS DE SAINT-LOUP; his uncle the BARON DE CHARLUS, the most haughty and the most debased personage of the entire clan; the DUC AND DUCHESSE DE GUERMANTES, neighbors both in Combray and in Paris; and the PRINCE AND PRINCESSE DE GUERMANTES, who occupy the pinnacle of Paris aristocracy and whose "world" Marcel finally enters. MLLE DE SAINT-LOUP, daughter of Robert de Saint-Loup and Gilberte Swann, appears briefly at the end of the novel. Swann's way and the Guermantes's way unite in her youthful form.

Beyond these clearly defined groupings there are several looser sets of characters. The three major artists— BERGOTTE, a writer; VINTEUIL, a composer; and ELSTIR, a painter—exert a profound intellectual influence on the action and, through their works, on three of the principal love affairs. They do not know each other, and they stand apart from the three performing artists: MOREL, a violinist; and LA BERMA and RACHEL, both actresses. Morel becomes deeply entangled in the story through sexual intrigue.

The remaining personages do not really form a category. MONSIEUR and MADAME VERDURIN belong to the wealthy bourgeoisie and have immense (and successful) social ambitions. DR. COTTARD lends his medical renown and preposterous conversation to their little group of friends. ALBERTINE, captured and kept but never fully possessed, occupies more of Marcel's attention than any other single character. The MARQUIS DE NORPOIS is the perfect ambassador; JUPIEN, his counterpart at the other end of the spectrum, is the ultimate functionary of vice.

Approximately eight great love affairs establish powerful and lasting links between certain of these characters (see Diagram III). Five involve Marcel, and three introduce other couples. The two sets alternate so that the first-person account of one of Marcel's loves is usually followed by the third-person account of another couple. The passionate yet never sullied love between Marcel and his mother and grandmother is fully introduced before the long arabesque-like curve of the affair between Swann and Odette. Then, like a juvenile echo of "Swann in Love," we are immersed in Marcel's adolescent love for Gilberte. Later he shyly and fruitlessly follows the Duchesse de Guermantes through the streets. (For the sake of simplicity I omit Marcel's general infatuation with the band of young girls on the beach at Combray. A season later his sentiments converge on one of them: Albertine.) The next love to appear is Saint-Loup's prodigal passion for the actress Rachel, whose talent is almost equal to her ambition. Marcel's jealous attachment to Albertine, the girl who came up out of the sands of Balbec, lasts through four volumes. Meanwhile, Charlus has pawned what remains of his reputation for the handsome, philandering violinist Morel. To these six one

III. COUPLES

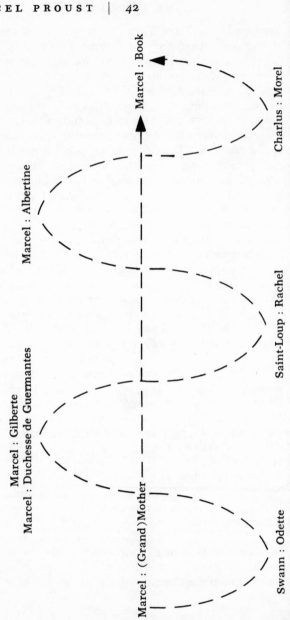

must add a seventh case, which is really double. During the long central sections of the novel Marcel seems to be in love with his own social success, even though he is aware of the vanity and superficiality of his surroundings. Then in the final volume his narcissism gives way to the urgency of a literary calling—his last and true love.

The society scenes with their ritualized pomp and gossip complement the exasperated intensity of the love affairs (see Diagram IV). These dinners and receptions and parties make up about a third of the book and lie along a gradually ascending social curve that finally turns back on itself. In the first volume Swann attends both a pretentious bourgeois dinner party at the Verdurins, at which the hostess directs her guests like performing animals, and an elegant musical soirée given by the Marquise de Saint-Euverte. Marcel's social progress begins humbly on the evening ex-Ambassador Norpois dines with his parents. Later, sitting in the orchestra during a charity evening at the Opéra, he watches the godlike Guermantes assembled in their box. Two receptions given by the Marquise de Villeparisis, a dinner with the Duc and Duchesse de Guermantes, and finally a soirée given by the Prince and Princesse de Guermantes, carry him to the pinnacle of aristocratic society in Paris and of his social ambitions. After this, social elevation becomes blurred by the intermingling of characters and castes. Twice Marcel attends major events at the Verdurins'. As time goes on their social chic and their wealth rival the status of the Guermantes. The most rewarding musical performance in the entire book takes place in their salon. Ultimately the astounding remarriage between the Prince de Guermantes and Mme Verdurin *veuve* transforms the social terrain to prepare for the last great reception, the novel's finale where all opposites meet.

Another third of the *Search* consists of passages of solitary meditation on perennial themes: childhood and

IV. SOCIETY SCENES

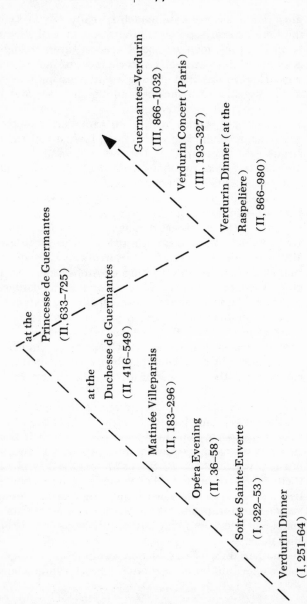

Verdurin Dinner
(I, 251–64)

Soirée Sainte-Euverte
(I, 322–53)

Opéra Evening
(II, 36–58)

Matinée Villeparisis
(II, 183–296)

at the
Duchesse de Guermantes
(II, 416–549)

at the
Princesse de Guermantes
(II, 633–725)

Verdurin Dinner (at the
Raspelière)
(II, 866–980)

Verdurin Concert (Paris)
(III, 193–327)

Guermantes-Verdurin
(III, 866–1032)

sleep; love, death, and time; art and morality. These psychological and philosophical thoughts cannot be described as detachable or extraneous. They enter the action as subtly and vitally as dreams shadow our waking life. It is essential to the mood and movement of the novel that it should open and close as its does with a sustained reflective passage by the undivided *I*. Marcel's thoughts on sleep, for example, are acts of mind which affect his development as much as any acts of love or social behavior.

THE PLOT

Proust's story does not emerge steadily from his text like news on a ticker tape. The narrative current is highly intermittent. Incidents collect in a series of great pools, like the social scenes just discussed. These pools engulf the landscape and give the impression of near motionlessness while we plumb the depths. Then, usually with little transition, we are carried to another wide basin of incident. Each of these pools has a geographical setting and, with the exception of "Swann in Love," covers a surprisingly short time interval. Usually it is a single season represented by a few crucial days. They are really pools of imperceptibly flowing time. The Narrator means more than mere topography when he refers to "the Combray basin" (III, 968), for that quiet body of time turns out to be an expanding universe that encroaches on all others.

Three significant sections stand outside these pools. The seven pages that open the book and the fifteen that close it frame the story by presenting it first as dream and last as art. Spanning the center of the novel is located a third sequence split into two parts that form an internal frame: the grandmother's death and (many months and four hundred pages later) Marcel's delayed realization of his loss (II, 314–15, 755–63). He experiences the full force of "intermittence of heart." The maturity Marcel attains after this rite of passage is incomplete and transitory, for it occurs in the midst of powerful distractions. Yet it reintroduces the almost forgotten forces of death and memory. This double incident holds the action in place from within, a recall to mortality in the middle of a story that is turning strongly toward frivolity.

In summarizing the plot now, I shall try above all to sketch the large movement of the action as it flows from pool to pool. It seems practical not to follow all Proust's divisions, which are makeshift or misleading at a few points, but to deal with large-scale, coherent bodies of event. Parts two and eight in the scheme followed below serve as intervals or intermissions. Though essential for spacing and timing, they fall outside the main action.

1. COMBRAY (I, 3–187). An unnamed Narrator of uncertain age is writing about himself in the first person. Yet he seems to be cut off from himself and from his past, out of which he can genuinely remember as his own only one vivid scene. One night during the Narrator's childhood (we shall call the boy Marcel), Monsieur Swann's company at dinner led Marcel's mother to refuse to come upstairs to kiss him goodnight. In protest, he kept himself awake until Swann had gone. She then relented, read to him, and spent the night in his room. Surprised, Marcel almost regretted her decision, which the Narrator calls "a first abdication" (I, 38). But this is all the Narrator can recall until, suddenly and unexpectedly, stimulated one day by the savor of a *madeleine* cake dipped in tea, he recovers the whole panorama of his childhood summers in the village of Combray. There, Marcel lived surrounded by older members of his family, according to the established routines of village and domestic life, discovering the pleasures of walking and eating and reading. Gradually his idyllic security is undermined by experiences that lead beyond "the drama of going to bed." People show unexpected and even contradictory sides. He sees they have no adequate way to

express their feelings. Meanwhile, Marcel becomes deeply aware of "the two ways" or paths that divide the village: one goes to the distant estate of the aristocratic Guermantes family, the other to Swann's house. Both ways whisper alluringly to the boy, drawing him away from his own lowly path. He feels the first stirrings of a literary vocation, along with an even stronger despair of ever becoming a writer.

2. SWANN IN LOVE (I, 188–382). Dropping back almost a generation, the Narrator relates in the third person the love affair between the Jewish man of the world, Swann, and the cocotte, Odette. She is really not his type of woman at all, yet his esthetic imagination propels him slowly through a powerful cycle of attraction toward this ordinary and enigmatic woman. Though he usually travels in the highest society, Swann begins to frequent the bourgeois Verdurin circle, where Odette is welcome and where he is finally humiliated in punishment for his lofty connections. His jealousy of Odette grows to pathological proportions before he begins a slow recovery. One assumes they will drift apart. Yet when they reappear in the narrative, they have married and had a daughter.

3. PARIS: GILBERTE SWANN (I, 383–641). As a boy playing in the Champs-Elysées gardens Marcel falls in love with Gilberte, the daughter of Swann and Odette. He also feels a strong fascination for the society of the father and mother. His love goes through an evolution similar to that of Swann's love for Odette and finally fades. Meanwhile, he is introduced to the charm of the theater, to sexual satisfaction, to the restraints imposed by his own poor health, and to literary eminence as embodied in the successful author, Bergotte. Marcel becomes increasingly aware of the difficulty of attaining happiness and of the unpredictable nature of human character.

4. BALBEC AND THE YOUNG GIRLS (I, 642–955). Now in his teens, Marcel goes with his grandmother for the

summer to Balbec, a fashionable resort on the English Channel. The Marquise de Villeparisis is staying in the same hotel. This former schoolmate of the grandmother's is a lady of high birth and scandalous past. Through her Marcel now meets the Baron de Charlus, as change-able as he is haughty, and her nephew, Robert de Saint-Loup. This elegant and intelligent young man is about Marcel's age; against all expectations they become the best of friends. Both Charlus and Saint-Loup belong to the Guermantes family. Yet for Marcel these summer days beside the beach focus increasingly on a somewhat rowdy band of young girls with bicycles, and then on one of them in particular, Albertine, apparently their leader. Her free behavior carries a hint of license and even of vice. After observing her for weeks, Marcel meets her in the studio of the painter Elstir, whose work he begins to understand and admire. When, at the end of his stay, Marcel tries to kiss Albertine in his hotel room, he fails ignominiously. Her true nature seems impenetrable, and he cannot even ascertain his own feelings toward her.

5. ENTERING THE GUERMANTES'S WORLD (II, 9–750). Back in Paris, Marcel and his family move into an apart-ment that belongs to the Duc and Duchesse de Guer-mantes and overlooks their town house. He has seen the Duchess once in Combray during a church service. She struck him at first as ugly. Yet, as he watched her across the church, she seemed to assume the symbolic beauty of her name. He now falls awkwardly in love and schemes shamelessly to meet her. For this purpose he goes to visit her nephew, Saint-Loup, who is doing his military service in Doncières. Robert is very friendly, yet remains guarded about his Guermantes relatives. He takes Marcel to lunch in Paris with his mistress, Rachel, and to one of her rehearsals. They go on to a reception at Mme de Villeparisis's, where Marcel finally does meet the Duch-ess. He also again sees the Baron de Charlus, who takes a curiously personal interest in him.

After this first glimpse of the Guermantes's world, Marcel's grandmother dies at the end of an exhausting ten-day agony.

Marcel's initiation into society continues, but along two complementary paths he had not foreseen: elegance and vice. Attending a dinner given by the Duke and Duchess, Marcel is first dazzled by the artistocratic guests, including the Princesse de Parme, then disappointed by the mediocrity of their conversation and behavior, and finally re-enchanted by the historical and genealogical patina of their mere names. Late that night Marcel visits Charlus, as invited, and is received in an ambiguous, almost violent manner. He cannot fathom the reasons. However, a few months later he watches from a window while Charlus picks up another man in the courtyard of their house. Marcel finally realizes that the Baron is a homosexual.

Marcel's ultimate advance into the Guermantes's society associates elegance and vice even more dramatically. At a huge evening reception at the Prince and Princesse de Guermantes', the eminences of Parisian aristocracy are laid out for Marcel's inspection in a crowded ceremonial portrait. Beneath the resounding titles, the magnificent surroundings, and the polite conversation, Marcel soon detects not only snobbery and political depravity (the Dreyfus Case is at its height), but also rampant homosexuality that taints some of the most honorable names. After this hollow realization of his social ambitions, Marcel finds that what he really wants more than anything is to have Albertine to himself.

6. BALBEC: ALBERTINE AND THE VERDURIN CLAN (II, 751–1131). The first night of his second visit to Balbec, Marcel is overwhelmed by the recollection of his grandmother and the meaning of her death. He sees Albertine regularly, and at the same time begins to suspect her of Lesbian inclinations. His jealousy makes increasing demands on her. The young couple attends the weekly dinner parties given by the Verdurins at the country

place they rent for the summer. Their circle of bourgeois friends has its own quaint customs and its own snobbery. The presence among them of the Baron de Charlus and of his protégé, the violinist Morel, adds a now familiar note of elegance and vice to these dinners. But as the summer goes on, Marcel finds that both Balbec and Albertine have lost their charm. Just at this point, he is appalled to discover that Albertine is a close friend of a notorious lesbian. He decides that he wants to marry her.

7. ALBERTINE IN PARIS: CAPTIVITY AND ESCAPE (III, 9–677). There is no marriage. That winter Albertine comes to live with Marcel in his apartment. Françoise and his mother hover disapprovingly in the background. He establishes a tyrannical routine in which he barely lets Albertine out of his sight without careful supervision. Spying and lying become their way of life, from which neither can escape. In order to pursue his suspicions about Albertine, Marcel goes to a reception at the Verdurins' Paris apartment. Charlus has arranged for Morel to give a concert that evening and has invited a small number of his aristocratic friends and relatives to attend this bourgeois affair. For Marcel the evening brings a great and lasting revelation of the pleasures of music. For most of the others, the evening devolves into a shameful public struggle over the dubious loyalty and real talent of Morel. Both the Guermantes and the Verdurins behave like boors. Unable to control either his homosexuality or his snobbery, Charlus is finally humiliated by his own protégé.

More than ever obsessed by jealousy and driven to deceit by a feeling of being himself a caged bird, Marcel hypocritically suggests separation to Albertine. He hopes that the prospect will strengthen her attachment to him. Instead, he wakes up one morning to find her packed and gone.

Marcel cannot bribe her to come back, nor can he

resolve his own contradictory feelings. A telegram announces that Albertine has been killed in a fall from a horse. Immediately afterward two letters from her arrive. In the one she wrote last, she asks—apparently sincerely —to come back to him. In Marcel's mind all sentiments and motives seem to crumble at this touch. Yet a jealous curiosity to know the "truth" about Albertine's private life continues to absorb him for some time. Slowly he gains a little distance, helped by the publication of one of his articles in the *Figaro* and by seeing Gilberte again. She has a new name and a new social being. Marcel also visits Venice with his mother. Certain earlier portions of the action now begin to drift back toward the surface of the story.

8. INTERMISSION (III, 677–854). Robert de Saint-Loup and Gilberte marry and are unhappy. Robert turns out to be a homosexual and neglects his wife. Marcel goes to visit Gilberte at Tansonville, the estate where Swann had lived near Combray. The village and its surroundings have lost their magic. One night he reads a passage in the Goncourt brothers' journal about the Verdurin salon in days past. The aura of their prose convinces him once again that he will never become a writer. While at Tansonville, Marcel discovers that the two "ways" which seem to lie in totally opposed directions do in fact join farther out in the countryside, just as the marriage of Gilberte and Robert has united two alien elements of society.

The war now interrupts the story. Marcel makes several long stays in a rest home outside Paris. During his rare visits to the city he learns how wartime conditions are transforming everyday life and the social hierarchy. Saint-Loup dies a hero at the front. Charlus descends further than ever into vice and self-degradation. Only Françoise survives, barely changed by age, the eternal attendant.

9. TIME RECAPTURED (III, 854–1048). Many years

later, Marcel returns to Paris resigned to a life of boredom and indifference. An engraved invitation to a reception given by the Prince and Princesse de Guermantes reawakens a little of the original spell of that name. Marcel finds no reason to deprive himself of the frivolous pleasure of seeing all those people again. When he arrives at the Guermantes's house and while he waits in the study for a musical interlude to finish, an upsurge of familiar sensations washes over him. These sensations, resembling the *madeleine* incident of the opening pages, set off a great sunburst of memory reaching all the way back to his earliest childhood and his mother reading to him in Combray. Alone in the study, he meditates on the nature of art and literature and re-encounters what he has believed utterly lost: the vocation to write. His subject will be this very loss of his calling—and the rediscovery of it. Having found the shape of his book in his own erring life, he feels ready to begin work.

However, when he enters the salon and meets his acquaintances, his new optimism crumbles into dust, for he cannot recognize any of these people who are, in effect, the substance of his past and the subject of his book. Age has transformed them all into grotesque puppets of their former selves. At the same time the very poles of society have reversed themselves through marriage, money, and natural evolution. The Princesse de Guermantes is no one else but—in her third marriage— Mme Verdurin. Stunned, Marcel recovers himself only when he meets Mlle de Saint-Loup, Gilberte's daughter, who fuses in her flesh the two ways of his childhood and renders visible the intervening years. Reconciled to time and to his own place both in it and outside it, Marcel at last resolves to write the book he has carried within him, and avoided, for so long. It will embody his response to time. He sets to work, troubled only by the realization that he has little time left in which to complete his task.

After a long life of false starts and distractions, a man discovers that he can after all reach a goal he gave up while still a boy: to write a novel. For the purpose he renounces the vanities of life and society, but only after having experienced them and learned from them. On the threshold of death he chooses art.

It is not a complicated plot in spite of its length. Marcel attains true mortality by assuming both its greatness and its puniness and by becoming his own Narrator. The story does not arrange the world into opposed forces vying for victory. For Marcel, all creatures, including those he loves most, are at the same time antagonists and accomplices. He struggles to see and to be—himself. When he holds his mother or Albertine captive, he has won no victory. There is only the long search, whose reward is the discovery that it all makes a story worth telling.

Do we believe such a story enough to respond to it? Though much modern criticism dismisses such considerations as entirely alien to literature, we can appropriately raise the question of verisimilitude. Proust's "rule" of writing to the point of exhaustion led to obvious extravagance. Some operatic or analytic passages overwhelm us. And how could any reader accept the coincidences on which the plot often turns? At the perfect moment Marcel moves into an apartment right in the Guermantes's back yard. Is it a fairy story? Charlus's great passion turns out to be for Morel, the son of Uncle Adolphe's valet and an acquaintance of Marcel's. Marcel is even on the scene and watching through the train window when Charlus picks up Morel on the platform. Yet Proust's universe, including Paris, is so small, so provincial even, that such events seem to belong. They were bound to happen. There is a similar inevitability about the characters as well. Like Goya and Daumier, Proust created devastating caricatures without sacrificing the complexity and humanity of his personages. Few of us have known people so distinguished and so depraved as Charlus, or so alluringly evasive as Albertine. Psychologically one of the most extravagant situations is Marcel's obsessive fascination with the name and nature of the Guermantes. He has a veritable love affair with a noble family. Yet in context, these portrayals achieve the unforgettable truth of fiction.

Homosexuality poses a more serious problem. It motivates Charlus, Saint-Loup, Mlle Vinteuil, Albertine (probably), Gilberte (possibly), the Prince de Guermantes, Morel (who is bisexual), and a large number of people in all strata of society. Proust would seem to be working with a set of characters so prone to homosexuality as to compromise the value and appeal of the novel. Not all of Charlus's harangues on the subject deserve the space they occupy. But it is worth noting that Proust, unlike Gide, never treated homosexuality as a higher form of love. He portrays it either as a condition determined by natural biological forces or as a taint, an unfortunate flaw in the distribution of human traits. And he sometimes acknowledges his obsession by releasing it in a scene of Rabelaisian exaggeration, like the first reception at the Prince and Princesse de Guermantes's.

Despite its extravagances, the *Search* remains a convincing portrait of an era. Certain details are priceless. When he begins going to exclusive parties, Marcel is utterly confused by the fad among the chic men of leaving their hats on the floor instead of consigning them to a footman. The descriptions of the telephone, automobile, and airplane in their early days have astonishing freshness, both documentary and poetic. More important is the fact that Proust inherited from Stendhal and Balzac a sensitivity to the process of social change. One gets the feeling that he takes time to paint the mores of Combray and of the Guermantes and Verdurin clans—three contrasting spheres of life—in order to be able to display the revolving motion that will gradually shift everyone's relative position. Yet the change does not obliterate all continuity. Though an era may be closing, the generations come and go in a cyclic movement that re-creates as much as it destroys. The wheel of fortune remains.

In living through the incidents I have summarized, Marcel reacts to more than society at large. He enacts a three-way conflict. We see him first shaped and defined by his family, who surround him with love yet never fully understand him. We see him reaching out yearningly toward society—society both in the form of an aristocratic caste which for a time he admires and envies, and in the form of men and women he seeks to know as individuals and possibly to love and possess. And we see him retreating increasingly within himself to find a quiet domain from which to observe others covertly yet understandingly. A great steady eye, he watches, trying never to condemn family or society, but letting us behold all the ways in which they fail him. In the end he does not fail us, or himself. For he tells his story in full.

The Comic Vision

iii

By one of the essential conventions in the
Search, Marcel remains innocent for a long time.
"Innocent" is of course a relative term. This
tender young boy catches on very early to what
makes the world go round. Not unlike his invalid
Aunt Léonie, he learns to bend his mother and
his grandmother to his will. Françoise, the family
cook and retainer, shows him that even a stern
code of conduct compromises with reality. And
Marcel contrives to spy on some juicy goings-on
in Combray and to pick up all available scandal
and gossip about the guests at the Grand Hôtel
in Balbec. Yet the way the story is told implies
that all worldly wisdom belongs to the Narrator
and that Marcel drifts wide-eyed through the
wicked world as a kind of cultivated cherub. Even
though Marcel's age is not made clear, the scenes
where he supposedly fails to comprehend the

Baron de Charlus's homosexual signaling in Balbec are disingenuous. But innocence has its limits. With a dramatic sense of timing not easily discernible behind the slow-moving narrative, Proust finally stages the great reversal. Approximately halfway through the novel he places four pivotal scenes in which Marcel loses his youth, his innocence, and his illusions.[1]

The first of these four scenes, probably the most moving one in the entire book, is the week-long agony and death of the grandmother. The kindest, truest person in the story metamorphoses into a series of human and bestial figures before death lays her to sleep, restored to herself as a little girl. The event has a strong though delayed effect on Marcel. Henceforward, in spite of his mother's continuing solicitude, Marcel senses that he is alone and unprotected. Immediately following this death sequence, and almost without transition. Albertine visits him in his apartment and yields to his desire, thus confirming his earliest sexual experience. A long society scene intervenes before the third climactic sequence: Marcel happens to observe the startling encounter between the Baron de Charlus and Jupien and comprehends at last that they are homosexuals. This recognition scene reveals a whole new world to Marcel; the Narrator compares him to Ulysses, who at first did not recognize Pallas Athena. That same evening, Marcel achieves the ultimate social honor of being received at one of the elegant evening receptions given by the Prince and Princesse de Guermantes. The account of that event—a one hundred fifty-page novella in itself—describes Marcel's loss of any last shred of belief that these "aristocrats" have something special or godlike about their persons and their lives. Despite their prestigious names,

[1] His virginity slipped away earlier, first in a clumsy encounter with an anonymous cousin, then in a *maison de passe* with Bloch (I, 575–78). Though these incidents "opened a new era" in his life (I, 711), the narrative does not fully register them until later.

they are as stupid, as self-centered, and as unhappy as
the rest of the world. Furthermore, they are even more
racked than others by the vice of snobbery, from which
one might think they could free themselves.

Thus Marcel's eyes are finally opened. This succession
of scenes turns Marcel away from his social climbing
and back toward his highly unsatisfactory yet absorbing
relationship with Albertine. The respective themes of
these four passages—death, love, vice, and social behavior—give them a distinctness that is reinforced by
the settings and the characters. Yet they share a common attitude toward experience, an understanding of
which I consider crucial to a responsive reading of the
novel. In order to bring out this aspect of Proust's work,
I shall examine all four scenes, beginning with the
shortest, Albertine's visit.

Late one afternoon in Paris as Marcel lies moping
on his bed, Albertine walks in unannounced. He finds
her changed since the previous summer, more sophisti-
cated. She responds to his advances, letting him kiss
her. The copious yet discreet narrative implies that their
caresses lead to further satisfactions, though apparently
not coitus. After a long, banal conversation about mutual
acquaintances and a fond good-by, Albertine leaves.
Summarized in this bare form, the incident promises
very little more than the commonplaces of sex. Let's see
what Proust has done with it.

When Albertine walks in on him, Marcel is thinking
quite lascivious thoughts, not about Albertine but about
another attractive girl from Balbec from whom he ex-
pects a message that evening. Two hours later when
Albertine leaves, Marcel will not commit himself to a
time to see her again. The other girl is still very much
on his mind, and he wants to keep his time open. Thus
the scene is framed in carnal desire, but carefully de-
flected so that Albertine's entrance comes both as a
total surprise and as perfectly appropriate to the mood.

We are reminded, however, that when Marcel first tried to make a pass at Albertine the previous summer in what looked like a perfect setup in his hotel room, she literally pulled the cord on him and rang for help. Will she respond now? The real question, the old refrain of every unexpected or long-delayed encounter with her, is: who is Albertine? Marcel stumbles about among sensual memories of Albertine in Balbec and present realities. "I don't know whether what took possession of me at that moment was a desire for Balbec or for her" (II, 351). He decides in any case that he is not in love with Albertine and wants no more than a simple, peaceful satisfaction from her presence.

But now he notices her language, the expressions she calmly produces from the new "social treasure" she has accumulated since the previous summer. Marcel makes a number of "philological discoveries" about her vocabulary. They provide the "evidence of certain upheavals, the nature of which was unknown to me, but sufficient to justify me in all my hopes" (II, 356). Marcel is indeed reading Albertine like a book.

> "*To my mind* [Albertine said], that's the best thing that could possibly happen. I regard it as the perfect solution, the stylish way out."
> All this was so novel, so manifestly an alluvial deposit leading one to suspect such capricious wanderings over terrain hitherto unknown to her, that, on hearing the words "to my mind," I drew her down on the bed beside me (II, 356).

Marcel has interpreted the signs correctly. If one is familiar with the way Proust moves calmly away from such moments and continues as if from another planet, the next sentences will come naturally.

> No doubt it does happen that women of moderate culture, on marrying well-read men, receive such expressions as part of their dowry. And shortly after

the metamorphosis which follows the wedding night, when they start paying calls. . . .

The sentence goes on for twenty lines. Having succeeded in maneuvering Albertine onto the bed. Marcel has wits enough about him only to try the "I'm not ticklish" approach. Albertine cooperates and, as they shift into position, asks considerately if she isn't too heavy. Then it happens.

As she uttered these words, the door opened and Françoise, carrying a lamp, walked in.

Albertine scrambles back to a chair. It is not clear whether Françoise has been following every move from outside the door or is simply bringing in the lamp at the usual hour. In the two-page examination of this interruption, we learn that Françoise's smallest actions constitute a moral language inflicting her code of values on everyone around her. She emerges convincingly from the analysis as the mythological figure of "Justice Shedding Light on Crime." Caught practically *in flagrante delicto*, Marcel tries to carry it off.

"What? the lamp already? Heavens, how bright it is." My object, as may be imagined, was by the second of these exclamations to account for my confusion, and by the first to excuse my slow reactions. Françoise replied with cruel ambiguity, "Do you want me to sniff it out?"
". . . snuff?" Albertine murmured in my ear, leaving me charmed by the lively familiarity with which, taking me at once for master and accomplice, she insinuated this psychological affirmation in the form of a grammatical question (II, 360).[2]

When Françoise leaves, Albertine is ready for action again. But not so Marcel. There is a precedent. Swann,

[2] Moncrieff translated Françoise's faulty subjunctive, "*Faut-il que j'éteinde?*" as "Do you want me to extinglish it?" Albertine supplies, "—guish!"

about to kiss Odette, tries to delay things in order to take full cognizance of what is happening. (See the passage quoted in the note on p. 26.) He senses something momentous and final in the act they are about to perform. Marcel holds off for similar reasons, about which we learn in some detail. Unhurriedly he rehearses the successive stages of their acquaintance and tries to reconstruct "this little girl's novel"—that is, her life beyond his ken. Knowing that it is now possible to kiss Albertine means more to Marcel than acting on the opportunity; his principal concern seems to be to breathe back into her person all the "mystery" she once carried so that, in kissing her cheeks, he will be kissing "the whole Balbec beach" (II, 363). Next comes a short disquisition on kissing and the dubious prospect of knowing anything by lip contact. We are now fifteen pages and probably an hour's reading time into the scene, and there would seem to be no way of spinning things out much longer. Marcel has her where he wants her, except that the old refrain never ceases: who is Albertine? I quote with only a few cuts.

> To begin with, as my mouth began gradually to approach the cheeks which my eyes had tempted it to kiss, my eyes, in changing position saw a different pair of cheeks; the throat, studied at closer range and as though through a magnifying glass, showed a coarser grain and a robustness which modified the character of the face.
>
> Apart from the most recent applications of the art of photography—which can set crouching at the foot of a cathedral all the houses, which time and time again, when we stood near them, appeared to reach almost the height of towers. . . . [ten more lines on photography] I can think of nothing that can so effectively as a kiss evoke out of what we believed to be a thing with one definite appearance, the hundred other things which it may equally well be, since each is related to a no less legitimate view of it. In short,

just as at Balbec Albertine had often appeared different to me, so now . . . [here seven lines to say that
such slow motion really serves to pass very rapidly
in review all the different impressions one has had
of a person] . . . during this brief passage of my lips
toward her cheek, it was ten Albertines that I saw;
she was like a goddess with several heads, and whenever I sought to approach one of them, it was
replaced by another. At least so long as I had not
touched her head, I could still see it, and a faint
perfume reached me from it. But alas—for in this
business of kissing our nostrils and eyes are as ill-
placed as our lips are ill-shaped—suddenly my eyes
ceased to see; next, my nose, crushed by the colli-
sion, no longer perceived any fragrance, and, without thereby gaining any clearer idea of the taste of
the rose of my desire, I learned from these unpleasant
signs, that at last I was in the act of kissing Albertine's cheek (II, 364–65).

Notice, among other things, that it is never directly
recorded in the testimony given here that Marcel kisses
Albertine. At the crucial moment, he literally loses his
senses. She vanishes. Consciousness cannot track experience to its lair. It must wait outside while another being,
blind but active, performs a deed that the consciousness
then reconstructs *ex post facto* from flimsy evidence.
The question "Who is Albertine?" pales to triviality
beside its counterpart: "Who am *I*?" But here Proust
has done two things simultaneously. He has shown how
sheer awareness, self-reflexiveness, erodes the reality of
any action, even, or rather particularly, when we attach
great significance to it; and he has written a superb
pastiche of his own style, a savage-sympathetic blow-up
of all the gestures with which he usually introduces us
to reality and its bitter disappointments. The relaxed
reader can be amused both by Marcel's resounding defeat of his own purposes *as he achieves them*, and the
Narrator's detachment from his own involuted narrative.

This "Kissing Albertine" sequence will bear sustained scrutiny. Most obviously, it dramatizes the dissociation of love, an idealized sentiment created by the imagination, from desire, focused on a material object. The passage also hints at Marcel's great yearning, in the midst of jealousies and disappointments, for the peaceable kingdom. He hopes Albertine will calm his life as his mother and grandmother were able to do. But few moments of serenity will in fact come from this budding affair. The action here echoes several other themes: the power of language to influence thought, the intermittent quality of character and identity, and the ironic timing of important events in our lives. But more important than this disparate content is the fact that all of it fuses not into a romantic or erotic scene but into a primarily comic incident. There is no element in the scene that fails to contribute to the mood of self-mockery leading to open laughter.

This is the shortest of the four sequences that turn Marcel's life toward the long plateau of maturity. It will be revealing to look at the other three in reverse order.

At the evening reception at the Prince and Princesse de Guermantes's sumptuous *hôtel particulier*, Marcel attains his social ambitions and, through one hundred fifty pages, observes the inflated emptiness and corruption of that society. The description of the characters recalls Daumier and even George Grosz. The Duc de Guermantes's crinkly hair, when he is angry, "seems to come out of a crater" (II, 683). The Marquise de Citry is "still beautiful, but barely suppressing a death rattle" (*"encore belle, mais presque l'écume aux dents"*) (II, 687). The comic element here is no mere matter of applied detail. From the start Marcel suspects that the invitation he has received to this chic affair is a hoax, and that he will be turned away at the door. His attempts to track down the origin of his invitation lead nowhere. Yet he cannot stay away. It gradually builds up to one of the great drolleries in Proust. The scene begins with an elaborate preparatory sequence about the head foot-man having been picked up the night before by an anonymous and generous gentleman who was in fact the Duc de Châtellerault. As it happens the Duke is just ahead of Marcel in line as they wait to have their names belted out to the guests by this same, now impos-ing footman. When the footman learns, from the man's own lips, his anonymous lover's identity, he "shouts [it] out with truly professional gusto tinged with intimate tenderness." Marcel now totters forward. His fears about the spuriousness of his invitation to this prestigious event have been built up for pages. I can only quote.

But now it was my turn to be announced. Absorbed in contemplation of my hostess, who had not yet seen me, I had not thought of the function—terrible to me, although not in the same sense as to M. de Châtelle-rault—of this footman garbed in black like a execu-tioner, surrounded by a group of lackeys in the most cheerful livery, stout fellows ready to seize hold of an intruder and cast him out. The footman asked me my name, I told it to him as mechanically as the con-demned man allows himself to be strapped to the block. Straightening up he lifted his majestic head and, before I could beg him to announce me in a lowered tone so as to spare my own feelings if I were not invited and those of the Princesse de Guermantes if I were, shouted the disturbing syllables with a force capable of shaking the very vaulting in the ceiling.

The famous Huxley (whose grandson occupies an unassailable position in the English literary world of today) relates that one of his patients stopped going out socially because often, on the actual chair that was pointed out to her with a courteous gesture, she saw an old gentleman already seated. She could be quite certain that either the gesture of invitation or the old gentleman's presence was a hallucination, for her hostess would not have offered her a chair that was already occupied. And when Huxley, to cure her, forced her to reappear in society, she felt a moment of painful hesitation when she asked herself if the friendly sign that was being made to her was the real thing, or if, in obedience to a nonexistent vision, she was about to sit down in public upon the knees of a flesh-and-blood gentleman. Her brief uncertainty was agonizing. Less so perhaps than mine. After the sound of my name, like the rumble that warns us of a possible cataclysm, I was bound, at least in order to plead my own good faith, and as though I were not tormented by any doubts, to advance toward the Princess with a resolute air.

She caught sight of me when I was still a few feet away and (in an action that left no further doubt about my being the victim of a conspiracy) instead of remaining seated, as she had done for her other guests, rose and came toward me. A moment later I was able to heave the sigh of relief of Huxley's patient, who, having made up her mind to sit down in the chair, found it vacant and realized that it was the old gentleman who was the hallucination. The Princess had just held out her hand to me with a smile (II, 637–38).

Proust narrates the incident with a precision of timing and flourish worthy of an acrobat balanced on top of a thirty-foot stack of tables. Twice he lets us think he is going to fall, first when he allows the Duke's subplot to take over, and later when he interrupts the story at the climax with the tantalizing Huxley digression. But he never loses control, and the story inches on. Basically Proust draws his effects here out of the double *I*. The enigmatic appearance of all unfamiliar things fills Marcel with anxiety and the Narrator with amusement. The resultant text shows us hallucination playing chase with perception, danger with detachment. We smile or chuckle each time the acrobat comes close to falling, though we remain apprehensive. After this opening, it is hard not to look for comedy in the rest of the scene.

We are not disappointed. Another comic motif helps

to bind together these one hundred fifty pages. After this reception at their brother's house, the Duc and Duchesse de Guermantes plan to go on to a costume ball where the Duke, an incorrigible ladies' man, will see his latest mistress. One of his cousins, we learn, is at death's door. The rules of decorum would normally keep them home, but they find an excuse to go to the Prince's reception anyway. When they return home between parties to change into their costumes, they learn that the cousin has finally died. All is lost. They can no longer ignore the proprieties. But the Duke, intent on his rendezvous, will not accept defeat. He girds himself to brush aside this obstacle with barely a nod toward decorum. "You're exaggerating!" he says resolutely to the two ancient ladies who have brought the news. He and the Duchess sally forth. The little motif of whether or not they will finally attend the costume ball winds through the entire episode. It is the same narrative device I mentioned earlier, a kind of refrain to lead the reader through a prolonged development. Yet this induced suspense over a triviality and its mechanical repetition has a comic effect that Proust exploits to the full. Other instances carry a similar effect. Aunt Léonie's whole day hangs on finding out from Eulalie whether Mme Goupil made it to mass on time, yet when Eulalie finally visits her, she forgets to ask. Likewise, the elaborate leads about the Baronne de Putbus's sexy chambermaid are finally shown to be pure anecdotal prank, for not only does Marcel fail ever to locate this alluring creature, but he and we also learn that he did once know her, long ago, as a child in Combray (III, 307). In the scene above, the Duke's costume-ball motif displays the unwavering selfishness of Marcel's protectors in high society and provides a sardonic commentary on all the magnificence.

It is natural enough that such society scenes should be decked out in comic accouterments. But there's something more disturbing and complex in the third of the four scenes I am examining. In it we learn, beyond a doubt, that Charlus is an active and obviously experienced homosexual. Proust warned his prospective editors that the scene was shocking—as indeed it was over fifty years ago. Out of sight in the stairway, Marcel watches Charlus and Jupien identify and approach one another in the courtyard and finally retire for half an hour to an inside room. Comic details and lines keep cropping up, though they remain a quiet obbligato. (At one point Jupien, suspecting Charlus may be a bishop, is himself scandalized.) Proust asks us to see the scene in three perspectives: as the demonstration of a set of scientific laws of attraction, here presented in precise botanical terminology; as a scene having a special kind of esthetic tone, comparable to the music of Beethoven; and as a comedy of shifting identities. The weave is very tight, and he maintains a careful balance among the three. The Narrator is more explicit than usual. "This scene, moreover, was not positively comic, it was overlaid with a strangeness or, if you will, with a naturalness, whose beauty kept growing" (II, 605). Now Proust's book has no villain; his psychology is too subtle for so static a classification of character. Charlus increasingly grows into an evil genius. He abandons health, reputation, and fortune for his vices. Nevertheless, even in the depraved scene near the end of the book, where he is being flagellated by a young man in Jupien's male bordello, a curious innocence hangs over the events. We are told that Charlus really has a good heart. None of the hired hands is vicious enough to get any kick out of whipping the old man; they do it reluctantly, only for money. And in the penultimate moment when Marcel meets Charlus on the Champs Elysées after the latter has had a ravaging heart attack, Proust paints the semiparalyzed Baron both as an indomitable Lear and as a senile puppet bowing to old enemies at

Jupien's prodding. The basest vice is not excluded from the comic vision.

We can now move back to the first of the four crucial scenes. Proust brings to bear on the grandmother's death in her family's Paris apartment his broad medical knowledge and a devastating insight into what happens to people in the presence of death. These forty pages contain one of the most unsparing descriptions of a death agony in all literature. Her loss confronts Marcel with the full burden of selfhood. And the week-long sequence displays the heroism of the grandmother as she faces death and tries to sustain her disintegrating humanity, and the courage of Marcel's mother. Her grief surpasses words and gestures, and at the same time she must try to control a household gone mad. Everything is brought to bear on this test of mortality. Yet, against all odds, even this is essentially a comic scene, drawing on deep-seated traditions of danse macabre and gallows humor. Without comedy, the heroism would be strained and unconvincing. As things stand, the courage and dignity of the two afflicted women shine out through multiple layers of burlesque.

Most obviously there is Françoise whose devotion and feeling cannot be distinguished from peasant insensitivity. She keeps acting as if the whole affair were a special holiday, a *jour de gala* for which her most important mission is to have her mourning clothes properly fitted. Over everyone's objections, especially the victim's, Françoise wants to set the grandmother's hair. "By dint of repeatedly asking her whether she wouldn't like her hair done, Françoise managed to persuade herself that the request had come from my grandmother" (II, 333). The faithful servant never stops massacring the French language. Having no adequate way to express deep feelings in words, she comes out with this urgent signal of moral distress. "I've got this heavy feeling on my stomach" (II, 340).

Meanwhile, Proust keeps wheeling in unlikely visitors. When the still articulate grandmother refuses to see the specialist, he insists on examining everyone else in the household instead—and infects them all with head colds. Françoise is then distracted by an electrician whom she cannot bear to send away. She talks to him for a quarter of an hour at the back door just when she is needed in the sick room. The Duc de Guermantes arrives, insists on speaking to Marcel's stricken mother, and is unable to get over his own graciousness in visiting this bourgeois family. A mysterious and distantly related priest comes to read and meditate by the bedside; Marcel catches him peeking between the fingers he holds folded over his face. Finally, when the celebrated consultant, Dr. Dieulefoy, makes his ceremonial entrance *in extremis*, the text blurts it right out: "We thought we were in a Molière play" (II, 342). Indeed they are—in a Molière play written by Proust. Right up to the time one reaches the sudden surge of stage movements and missed cues that surrounds the actual death, laughter is one among the strong conflicting responses.

A MATTER OF TEMPERAMENT: THE OPENING STUMBLE

Proust is conventionally portrayed as a brooding figure, bedridden and sinister, given to devious sentiments and suspicious medications. Because his psychological analyses never move briskly but swing slowly back and forth like the long-stemmed neurasthenic water lilies he describes near Combray, we tend to find him solemn. Brevity is said to be the soul of wit; a work as lengthy as the *Search* must be directed toward high seriousness or gloom. Even sympathetic and intelligent critics have been blinded. "The normal, middle-distance view of human comedy," states Stuart Hampshire, "is altogether lacking in [Proust's] novel."

Proust had many vices, and at times his behavior

seems a little spooky. But no reliable account of his life could picture him as an old sober-sides. Many of his most revealing letters, once past the ingratiating phrases and the self-deprecation, take on a bantering tone. He seemed to nourish his restless intelligence on a diet of gossip about everyone he knew, including those closest to him; yet his curiosity was not so much malicious as finely sensitive to all human foibles. In a letter to Antoine Bibesco he reports this telephone conversation with the Marquis Louis d'Albufera, an unbookish young rake who fascinated Proust:

"Well, Louis, have you read my book?"
"Read your book? Did you do a book?"
"Of course, Louis, I even sent it to you."
"Ah . . . Well, if you sent it to me, my dear Marcel, I've surely read it. Only I'm not sure I received it."

Proust apparently had a special propensity for *le fou rire*—uncontrollable laughter. Lucien Daudet, a close friend from Proust's early twenties, makes much of the fact that even in later years he and Proust sometimes could not contain themselves. It happened not only when they were tweaked by a specific comic incident or expression, but often because, in a mental set created by an unexpected shift in their sensibility, *everything* suddenly became hugely funny. It is a precious state of mind.

Careful attention to biographical accounts reveals a gay, often mischievous Proust, endowed with tremendous verbal spontaneity. He carried his friends along with him in perpetrating elaborate verbal pomposities, like saying "Albion" for England and "our loyal troops" for the French Army.

The waggishness that runs through Proust's conversations and correspondence entered his literary works slowly. His first book, *Pleasures and Days*, attempts only the gentlest of comic effects. In the heaped up materials of the projected novel *Jean Santeuil*, the comic touches are much more frequent, yet still tentative. The most amusing sequence comes at the very start, where the young narrator describes and implicitly ridicules his own excitement on discovering that a famous author is living in the same rustic hotel on the Brittany coast. The whole section mocks the literary convention, to which it belongs, of the manuscript found in a bottle. Fully matured, the same attitude guides the masterful *Pastiches*, which Proust wrote for practice and for publication. They are so fully controlled that it is impossible to do them justice by fragmentary quotation. Proust's sly mimicry of an author belongs to his text as a whole; its individual parts seem perfectly normal. The pastiches demonstrate that style as a self-conscious personal mode tends fatally toward the ridiculous. The greater the stylist, the more vulnerable he is to pastiche. Yet far from inhibiting Proust, that discovery apparently liberated him to write according to his own bent and face the consequences. He acknowledges the perils of a personal style by incorporating into the *Search* passages that function in part as self-parody. As I have tried to show, the "Kissing Albertine" sequence is one such passage. Proust referred to his published pastiches as "a matter of hygiene" (*CSB*, 690) which purges him of other writers' influence. Self-mockery helped him navigate among his own excesses.

The brooding and even grim image of Proust's work is inappropriate. Released from it, one soon discovers a novel overlaid with amusing scenes and details.[3] The

[3] The eighty pages (III, 478–558) in which Marcel, as if by sheer exercise of his mental powers, gradually recovers from the shock caused by Albertine's death, come closer than any other in the book to being devoid of humor. In fact the grimness of this section (in a letter to his editor Proust once described it as "the best thing I've written") provides a problematic reading on the extent of Marcel's trauma. In the case of the grandmother's death, the shock is long de-

benevolent Princesse de Luxembourg has difficulties adjusting to the social distance that separates her from Marcel. When he is presented to her, she almost pets him, like an animal at the zoo, out of sheer kindness. The celebrated wit of the Duchesse de Guermantes jeers at the world, and is itself jeered at in turn as self-centered and artificial. Verbal comedy, in fact, permeates every scene and every character, major and minor. Dr. Cottard is an unstoppable machine for producing the most cobwebbed cliché for any situation. Françoise's endless howlers prevent Marcel from ever taking his own language for granted. And she is helped by a small cast of characters whose principal role seems to be exclusively that of fracturing French. To the elevator boy in Balbec, Mme de Cambremer will never be anything but Mme de Camember—Mrs. Cheese. To process everything novel back into familiar terms is a form of intellectual deafness most prominently displayed in language. The elevator boy's director, a Rumanian émigré out of his depth in his adopted tongue, produces solid paragraphs of untranslatable barbarisms: *"fixure"* for "fixture," *"granulations"* for "gradations." Proust sometimes allows the director to carry on his word-scrambling for too long. Yet one cannot help laughing aloud.

There is a scene in which Mme Cottard falls asleep in her chair after a big dinner at the Verdurins' summer place. Proust rides the crest for three pages, obviously enjoying himself. Spoofing all his own earlier scenes about sleep, he runs through a learned medical discussion on the subject and has Dr. Cottard cruelly keep waking his wife to tell her it's time to leave, only to let her relapse again. When she finally comes up blinking out of the depths, she is still talking in her dream. The guests enjoy the performance.

---

layed, probably deeper, and surrounded by comic circumstances. Even in the "Albertine Is Dead" section, Aimé's work as a private detective for Marcel introduces some discreetly scabrous comedy (III, 515–16, 525).

"My bath is just right," she murmured. "But the feathers on the dictionary . . ." she cried, straightening up. "Oh, Good Lord, how foolish I am. I was thinking about my hat, and I must have said something ridiculous. Another minute and I would have dozed off. It's the heat from that fire that does it." Everybody began to laugh, for there was no fire (II, 962).

Mme Cottard looks ridiculous because she has confused waking and dreaming and produces the anomaly of "dictionary feathers" as a souvenir of her trip. But this little scene tucked away in the middle of the novel reveals unexpected links with the opening of the book. Both moments are located in the precarious zone between sleep and waking, and Mme Cottard's very human behavior sets the novel's first three sentences in a new light. Listen to them again. These are the first words Proust offers us, a subtle gambit, the flash of mental and physical movement which will influence every moment to follow.

For a long time I used to go to bed early. Sometimes, when I had barely put out my candle, my eyes would close so quickly that I did not even have time to say to myself, "I'm going to sleep." And half an hour later the thought that it was time to go to sleep would awaken me.

When we first see him, Marcel is as confused as Mme Cottard. His attention, his grasp of what he is and what he is doing, collapses under him. I interpret this incident as an epistemological stutter or stumble, deliberately placed ahead of all other incidents. It functions like a standard vaudeville routine: the curtain opens; an actor walks out on stage; before he can open his mouth, he trips hugely and barely saves himself from falling. Laughter. Proust's *I* does something very similar. He stumbles over his self-awareness before the book is under way. According to one scale of events, he regains his balance forty pages later as Marcel in the "Combray" section. According to another, more basic scale, the equilibrium of self-recognition does not occur until 3000 pages later. And even then Marcel, metamorphosed into the Narrator of his own life, is perched on grotesque stilts which reach back into his past and on which he can barely stand. Montaigne uses the same carnival metaphor in the closing lines of his last essay, "On Experience," and tells us to keep our feet on the ground. Proust does not shrink from portraying the elevations and pratfalls out of which our deepest insights may emerge.

THE USES OF THE COMIC

Beyond its own life as sheer exuberance and celebration, the comic has earned a place in "serious" literature through three potential roles: as social corrective, as relief from the tensions of plot or implacable fate, and as a vehicle for forbidden content. These categories will shed some light on Proust's practice.

What is excessively individual or conformist in us usually comes out as rigid, mechanical behavior. A natural Bergsonian, Proust brought on his characters both masked and revealed by their tics. Mme Verdurin has a sobbing ritualized laugh that betrays the artificiality of her feelings. Saint-Loup, though favored with elegance and *savoir-faire*, slips sideways through all doorways, as if he has something to hide. (He does.) Proust excels in depicting exaggerated, socially compromising conduct, but the corrective edge of the comic in the *Search* is constantly blunted by uncertainty about what represents appropriate behavior in a society coming apart before our eyes. The grandmother's death is a Molière play in that large portions of the action veer toward satire and even burlesque. But in Proust there is no assumed universe of harmonious manners to appeal to, no *juste milieu*.[4] Awkwardness is simply part of our lot. Corrective action will not avail.

Many of the comic elements I have cited earlier are undeniably diverting and may provide "relief" from a highly extended story. A superb two-page caricature of monocle styles in the middle of a social scene (I, 326–327) seems to serve such a purpose. Yet a monocle described by Proust reveals social manners as well as individual character. And from what could we be relieved by comic elements merely inserted or pasted on? For Proust has jettisoned most conventions of linear plot and character development. We are rarely sure of motivation and intention, or of where events are headed. When the Narrator proposes three or four possible explanations for what happens, and an equal number of possible results, a sense of dislocation and anomaly becomes the very ground out of which the action springs. This sense does not just raise its head at long intervals as "comic relief." As I have tried to show, it weaves tightly through scenes one would usually consider serious or emotional.

The third role conventionally assigned to comedy figures more importantly in the *Search* than the first two, and Proust explicitly recognized this function. By depicting a "depraved" character like Charlus as comic, ultimately as a mock-heroic figure, Proust seems both to pass sentence on him as a deviation from the norm,

---

[4] In a text not incorporated into the novel, Proust gave a notion of how far the comic sense of life, free of moral overtones, invaded his sensibility. He described Bergotte as leading an unrepentantly dissolute life, yet writing books which set very demanding moral standards. The morality of such people, the Narrator states, "makes the good consist in a sort of painful consciousness of evil . . . rather than in abstention from it" (Maurois, pp. 146–47). The revealing yet disturbing thing about this fragment is that Bergotte's friends find his inconsistent behavior, not in bad faith or hypocritical, but "comic."

and simultaneously to grant him pardon for that deviation. Charlus's vices look like a grotesque caricature,
and thus Proust sought dispensation for the forbidden
content he felt compelled to deal with. He wrote to the
publisher Fasquelle to say that nothing was really shocking in his novel, and then corrected himself in a parenthesis: "(or rather it is saved by the comic, as when the
concierge calls the white-haired Duke [sic, for "Baron"]
a 'big kid'. . . .)" As Freud insisted, in writing about wit,
the comic furnishes protective coloring for themes that
cannot be introduced without it. Social corrective and
comic relief do not help much in understanding the
Search, but the novel does rely sometimes on the camou-
flage effect of the comic.

From the start of the *Search* we are given the record
of a sensitive consciousness eager to discover and enter
the outside world of appearances, and apparently unable
to do so in any satisfactory way. Marcel remains confined inside a pliable but impenetrable membrane of
self-consciousness. Yet he cannot turn away from the
universe of attractive enigmatic beings that present
themselves outside his consciousness and his identity.
The comic element in the novel follows this division into
outward and inward.

In the external world the comedy arises from many
sources. The French critic Gilles Deleuze has recently
emphasized the way in which Proust presents people
inhabiting a world of signs and clues needing astute
interpretation. One result of this constant decoding, a
result Deleuze fails to bring out, is a parade of *gaffes*, a
comedy of errors. Marcel is forever getting his signals
switched and confusing identities. He even mistakes the
color of Gilberte's eyes and falls in love particularly with
her "azure" eyes, when in fact they are black (I, 140–
141). Yet there is no surer path to the truth than through
such foolish blunders. "An error dispelled gives us a new
sense" (II, 613).

Most tellingly, however, the comic tone in outward

events results from botched timing. Few things happen when expected, or as desired, or as might be appropriate. Usually things come too late; by the time their charms become available to him, Marcel has half lost interest in the haughty Guermantes family and in the person of Albertine. At other moments the timing is too perfect; the unlikely coincidences and windfalls which favor Marcel usually paralyze him. Both kinds of timing make him look ridiculous. Combined and reinforced, they persist into the novel's closing sequence, which relates Marcel's encounter with death.

After long absence from Paris, now aging more than he realized, Marcel attends the last great Guermantes reception. With difficulty he recognizes his old friends and, through them, the tortuous track of his own life. He resolves once and for all to sit down and write the book he has been carrying inside him all these years. Françoise, the only surviving witness, recognizes the change in him and at last "respected my work" (III, 1034). Immediately, however, Marcel finds himself blocked. The discovery of the essential truths about time that give him the confidence to begin his novel also makes him aware of his vulnerability to contingent time. For time can inflict death on him at any moment, wipe out "the precious deposits within him," and prevent him from completing his work. At the start of the book, Marcel fumbles his timing in falling asleep. At the close, he picks the wrong time to settle down to producing a work of art. Yet this worst of all threats is given detached, almost amused treatment.

> Now, by a bizarre coincidence, this carefully considered fear [of death] came alive in me at the moment when the idea of death had just recently become indifferent (III, 1037).

Marcel appears always out of step, always the victim as he confronts the external world.

Yet inwardly he remains undiscouraged in spite of all.
Resignation and lucidity give him strength. Self-deprecation is his form of courage. In later years he finds it
incredible that he should ever have bestowed special
status on the Guermantes clan. And it is even more
ludicrous that anyone, particularly a Guermantes, should
see merit *in him*.

> Later, I learned that the Guermantes believed that I
> belonged to a race apart, but a race that aroused their
> envy because I had merits unknown to me and that
> they prized above all others (II, 439).

Marcel cannot believe in his own accomplishments.
When he happens upon an article he wrote, finally published in the *Figaro*, he fails for a time to register the
fact. "I opened the *Figaro*. How annoying! The lead
article had exactly the same title as the article I had
sent them and that they hadn't printed yet" (III, 567).
Self-deprecation turns into slapstick when the Narrator
describes Marcel's first entrance into a very chic café.

> . . . I had to go in alone. Now, to begin with, once I
> had ventured into the revolving door, a device I wasn't
> accustomed to at all, I thought I'd never get out again
> (II, 401).

Such incidents have a theatrical flavor. Proust carries
the effect even further in the carefully planned double
incident of Mme Swann walking at noon in the Bois
de Boulogne surrounded by her reputation and her admirers. In the first version (I, 419–21), Marcel is "an
unknown young man whom no one noticed." Palpitating
yet resolute as he sees her approaching, acting on the
dubious basis of his acquaintance with Mme Swann's
daughter and his parents' acquaintance with her husband, "I raised my hat to her in so exaggerated a gesture
that she could not help smiling. People laughed." Though

merely an "extra" on the fringes of her performance, Marcel feels more pleasure than humiliation in accomplishing this exploit. A few years later, when Marcel has come to know Mme Swann quite well, the scene is restaged with Marcel placed inside the magic circle, under Mme Swann's parasol, talking confidentially with her, holding her jacket. Looking out at the public, he sees one or two unknown young men summoning up the courage to greet her. Then, in fascination, he watches the ceremonial entrance of the most elegant aristocrat of the era, historically the genuine article, the Prince de Sagan. "The Prince, turning his horse's head toward us as if for an apotheosis on stage, or in the circus, or in an old painting, addressed to Odette a grand, theatrical, almost allegorical salutation" (I, 640). It is all *performed* —both vivid and unreal, thus held far enough away for a subtle destructive element to seep in around the edges. When Marcel first greeted Mme Swann, people laughed. Now that he stands among the mighty, there is no open laughter. But having reached the apparent center of the universe in this scene of apotheosis, Marcel still seems vaguely out of place—and this time the others along with him.

At least this is how the Narrator paints things. And it may be evident how the double *I* of Proust's narrative helps create the novel's gently mocking tone. Marcel and the Narrator form a contrasting pair like comic and straight man—*clown et auguste*. Either one without the other would not hold our attention for long. Together they combine innocence and wisdom. The jokes are on Marcel, told by his alter ego, the Narrator, looking back on his former self. The syntax of the story carries inside it this enlarged and ultimately comic perspective of reflection and memory. That perspective cannot be peeled off the body of the narrative as incidental entertainment or social commentary. It constitutes one of the most human aspects of Proust's vision. This is a far cry from the gloomiest book ever written.[5]

---

[5] Among standard works on Proust, only those by André Maurois and Léon Pierre-Quint take time to consider his comic side. Neither does much more than introduce a chapter on how Proust achieves amusing effects through character, language and situation. Two scholarly-critical works have developed the subject along similar lines: Roland André Donzé, *Le Comique dans l'œuvre de Marcel Proust* (Neuchâtel, 1955), and Lester Mansfield, *Le Comique dans Marcel Proust* (Paris, 1953). Only Germaine Brée, in a chapter of *Marcel Proust and Deliverance from Time*, does justice to the pervasiveness and the organic role of comedy in the *Search*.

Proust's Complaint

IV

FALSE SCENTS

Like the youngest son in a fairy tale, Marcel is given three chances to succeed. He tries three solutions to the puzzle of life, and one after the other they fail. Of course it turns out in the end that he has won without knowing it, as if he had walked backward into paradise. The three magic stones, the three wishes he was allowed, come to naught. But since error recognized is a source of personal knowledge, the years of quest have not been wasted.

The first false scent leads to the Faubourg Saint-Germain, the quarter of Paris inhabited by the oldest families of the nobility. Marcel smells from far off the legendary amalgam of birth, title, and landed property that forms aristocratic society. It showed its last spark of life in France during the prewar years in which the *Search* is set. Marcel supposes that there is a fourth ingredient as well: nobility of character. Instead, he finds totally human lineaments exaggerated and distorted by the setting. The *prestige* (a key word in Proust) of the rich and titled turns to tinsel when approached close up.

After preliminary trials and rehearsals, Marcel enters the select domain on the evening he is invited to dine with the Duc and Duchesse de Guermantes. The Duke himself displaying his most considerate politeness meets him at the door. After visiting the collection of Elstir paintings, Marcel is presented to the Princesse de Parme. She seems to radiate a Stendhalian aura and a gentility all her own. Then, before Marcel can begin to identify the other guests, dinner is announced, the machinery starts, the Duchess circles the salon like a protective huntress to take his arm, and they enter the dining room "in a rhythm of exact and noble movements" (II, 434). At this point the action freezes, and the Narrator opens an unsparing fifty-page digression on the wit and politics of the Guermantes. Marcel tries to find some ground on which to resist his initial negative reaction to his hosts.

But just as in the case of Balbec or Florence, the Guermantes, after having first disappointed the imagination because they resembled their fellow men more than their name, could afterward, though to a lesser degree, hold out to one's intelligence certain distinguishing particularities (II, 438).

By the end of the dinner a hundred pages later, it is the remarkable genealogy of their names and the history of their titles that re-endows these vulgar citizens with fascination, with "their lost poetry" (II, 532).

Thus the prestige of the Guermantes and their kind survives essentially as an established form of *snobbery*. For Proust, snobbery is the great cohesive force that holds society together. He studies it tirelessly at every social level. The word itself covers two major attitudes or classes of snobbery. Proust contrasts them in a semi-mathematical formula while describing the Duchesse de

Guermantes when she still had the title of Princesse des Laumes.

> She belongs to that half of humanity in whom the curiosity the other half feels toward the people they don't know is replaced by an interest in the people they do know (I, 335).

The sentence bears expansion. Persons securely favored with high rank and wealth are prone to a snobbery of self-satisfaction, expressed in their exclusive attention to their own class and milieu. Those not so favored, but who aspire to social position, are prone to the snobbery of social envy, a desire to spurn their own class and milieu. Of course the snob rarely occurs in the pure state, without a tincture of the other category. Charlus "combined in himself the snobbery of queens and that of servants" (III, 598). Proust is using the word in the second sense when he refers to a woman as "snobbish even though a duchess" (III, 266). The varieties of *mondanité* gradually give Marcel an understanding of the springs and wheels that turn the social machine.

One of Proust's early titles for the first volume of his novel was "The Age of Names." He means *proper* names, of places and of people. Only such names seem to stand for "something individual and unique" (I, 387). The false scent of social success corresponds closely in the novel to the age of names. For years, what ignites Marcel's imagination is always in a name. A train timetable reads like poetry, just as a noble title has the magic power of "a fairy" (II, 11, 533). As times goes on, these names, the most eminent and effective vehicles for prestige, wither and almost die. The "semantic illusion" of social prestige, despite its poetic origins, hardens into the dry husk of snobbery.[1]

The second false scent is love, both as sentimental at-

---

[1] The best description and analysis of this "semantic illusion" can be found in "Proust et le langage indirecte," by Gérard Genette, collected in *Figures II* (1969).

tachment and as physical desire. The two can be distinguished, but neither leads to true gratification. Swann's
famous last words on the death of his love for Odette
catch the mood of disappointment.

> To think that I wasted years of my life, that I hoped
> to die, that I had my greatest love affair with a woman
> who didn't appeal to me, who wasn't even my type
> (I, 382).

Proust extends to the verge of solipsism what Stendhal
and Nerval knew about the imaginary subjective nature
of love. In his liaison with Albertine, Marcel makes his
own special variation of Swann's pattern. In both cases a
transformation takes place not unlike that which we
have seen modifying the dynamics of the social sphere
and turning respect for rank and honor into snobbery.
By a kind of psychological fate, love decays into the very
different yet equally powerful force of *jealousy*. It happens to Swann and Marcel (and to Saint-Loup and Charlus) before love has achieved fulfillment or equilibrium.
Why must it be so? It is as if the capacity of physical
actions and ordinary words to reach behind appearances
and touch another person fails us when we most need it.
Communication falls short—whereupon love and desire
yield to a kind of emotional envy which feeds on the pos-
sibility that the loved one is communicating better with
someone else. Given its head, the imagination then runs
away with everything. ". . . the mind goes to work; instead of a need one finds a novel" (III, 1022).

What disturbs many Proust readers more than his
uncompromising criticism of love is the fact that he does
not spare friendship. Gradually we are forced to perceive
that egotism, distraction from boredom, and insecurity
reign over the only friendship Marcel allows himself,
that with Saint-Loup. And the Narrator leaves no room
for doubt. Friendship tends to make us

> sacrifice the only real and incommunicable part of
> ourselves . . . to a superficial self which does not,

like the other one, find any joy in its own being, but is touched to find itself held up by external props, taken in and sheltered by an individual foreign to itself (II, 394).

Proust's correspondence and biography demonstrate the importance that friendship held for him and the steadiness with which he observed its rituals, if not its realities. Thus it is perplexing to read a letter he wrote in 1901 to Antoine Bibesco (who became one of his closest friends) upbraiding him for abusing the code of friendship and in the same breath affirming that friendship is "something without reality." We will simply have to live with the fact that profound skepticism about generally recognized sets of human feelings can coexist with a yearning for those feelings. In the *Search*, the Narrator's description of Marcel's long detour through the false promises of love and friendship is virtually congruent with the story itself.

The third false scent in the novel will be much harder to deal with than the other two, because it carries us into the domain of the intellectual and the esthetic. Not only did Proust's thinking in this area shift and evolve as he wrote, but he often presented and dramatized views opposed to those in which the Narrator ultimately puts his faith.

The third path of error is art—not all art, but art misconstrued and given false value. A dilettante and esthete in his youth, Proust developed his own convictions in the crucial period when he won his independence from Ruskin. In the postscript he added to his introduction to *The Bible of Amiens*, and in the later introduction to *Sesame and Lilies*, a series of references single out as "intellectual sin" what begins as a form of artistic "snobbery" (*CSB*, 183). This "essential infirmity of the human mind" (*ibid.*, 134) is attributed to Ruskin as well as to Montesquiou, Proust's two intellectual heroes at that time. They are guilty of esthetic "fetishism" (*ibid.*, 117), a veneration of the symbol instead of the reality it represents, a worship of esthetic beauty without approaching the "discovery of truth" (*ibid.*, 132) that gave it birth and significance. *Idolatry* is the word Proust finally settles on to carry his full condemnation of this esthetic attitude (*ibid.*, 129–41).

In the *Search* we are given so much varied discussion of art that it is difficult to sort out false or provisional attitudes from the deepest insights. The book closes with a great philosophical affirmation of art as a means of discovering and communicating truth. But art objects set up as fetishes, removed from life and from moral meaning, come under steady attack. A sensitive and intelligent amateur of the arts, Swann is nevertheless a victim of "idolatry of forms" (I, 852) because he tries to arrange his life—even his love life—according to the narrow beauty he sees in art. Bergotte, a genuine though limited artist in his writings, has, when he dies, a glimmering sense that he has taken the wrong course, that he has been "imprudent." Looking at a little yellow patch in the Vermeer painting he has gone to see ("That's how I should have written"), he has a heart attack.

> A celestial scales appeared to him which carried on one side his own life and on the other the little patch of wall that was so beautifully painted. He felt that he had imprudently given up the former for the latter (III, 187).

He had been a fetishist, and he dies as one. In the curious image that follows, his books are arranged by threes in bookstore windows, "like angels with unfurled wings . . . the symbol of his resurrection" (III, 188). But by now we know better. Such a resurrection can take place only among the cultists of esthetic idolatry. Proust's tone is deeply ironic. Bergotte had wasted his life and therefore compromised his art.

What I am arguing here differs from much prevailing criticism. Therefore, I shall document it further. Though there are long passages of conversation in the novel,

Marcel's words are rarely given in direct discourse. What he says is barely summarized, and often passed over in silence. (Possibly this is further evidence that we cannot be ourselves with others.) Exceptionally, Marcel is quoted at some length in a conversation with Charlus, who is bemoaning the wartime destruction of the Combray church. "The combination of surviving history and art that represents France at her best is being destroyed" (III, 795). (It also represents Marcel's childhood.) Charlus goes on to wonder whether the statue of Saint Firmin in Amiens has also been destroyed. "In that case," he adds, "the highest affirmation of faith and energy in the world has disappeared." Marcel raps his knuckles.

> "Its symbol, Monsieur," I answered. "And I adore certain symbols as much as you do. But it would be absurd to sacrifice to the symbol the reality it stands for. Cathedrals should be venerated until the day when, in order to save them, one would have to renounce the truths they teach. The arm of Saint Firmin raised in a gesture almost of military command, declared: Let us be broken if honor requires it. Do not sacrifice men to stones whose beauty has caught for a moment a few human verities" (III, 797).

There is no other passage quite like it in the book. The Author has thrust his head through the text in order to speak to us directly. In his desire to refute idolatry, he violates the conventions of his own work. As a character, Marcel is never so resolute and categorical as this speech suggests. Even the Narrator speaks more softly. In fact, Marcel inherits from Swann and Bergotte a sense of the privileged status and calling of art. Its elevated position has made it impossible for him to believe he could ever become an artist. How could he lift his lowly insights and impressions to the exalted regions of literature? Esthetic snobbery, or *idolatry*, has kept him from pursuing his own vocation.

Another illustration of this mental cramp of Marcel's occurs in the section early in the final volume where he reads himself to sleep over a passage out of the Goncourt brothers' journal. This scene, which includes Proust's masterful nine-page parody of the Goncourts' arty journalism, suddenly turns the action of the story back on itself, as when a passenger is startled to see the other end of his train while going around a curve. The false scents and lost quests seem to lead here, and produce a deep feeling of discouragement.

In the Goncourt "extract," Marcel finds himself reading about a dinner at the Verdurins. The apartment, the people, the stories are all familiar. Yet, as now described, they appear bathed in miraculous glow of literary and historic importance. The Goncourts have observed everything, right down to the elegant plates the meal is served on. Every detail of that life seems exciting and significant. In consequence, as he reads, Marcel feels everything tumbling down around his ears. He knew all these people. How could he have gone so far astray as to consider the Verdurins a couple of mediocre bourgeois social climbers and bores if they can inspire these lyric pages? The people he had classified as mere bit players (*figurants*) turn out, in the Goncourts' authenticating account, to be the leads (*figures*). The closing sentences of the passage describe Marcel's quandary as belonging both to life and to literature.

> . . . it amounted to wondering if all those people whom one regrets not having known (because Balzac described them in his books or dedicated his works to them in admiring homage, about whom Sainte-Beuve or Baudelaire wrote their loveliest verses) or even more if all the Récamiers and the Pompadours would not have struck me as insignificant people, either because of some infirmity in my nature . . . or because they owed their prestige to an illusory magic belonging to literature (III, 723; cf. II, 30).

Everything is now in jeopardy. Either Marcel has misjudged all the apparently tiresome and fraudulent people of fashion he knew and has been blind to their real importance; or else they are indeed as ordinary as they appeared and it is the magnifying, transforming power of literature that has raised them to an imaginary and fraudulent prestige.[2] He is unable to reject either alternative. Both ways, he loses. Marcel perceives that the Goncourts write as snobs and idolators, and that at the same time their mannered style affects his sensibility more forcefully than he would like. This lucid grasp of a contradictory dilemma affords him no comfort. It is precisely at this point in the story that Marcel takes refuge "for long years" in a *maison de santé* outside Paris.

Everything seems to go wrong for Marcel. Social success is empty. Love and friendship carries him not to the discovery of another person but into closer quarters with himself. Art may be a lie, getting in the way of reality. The passage about Marcel reading the Goncourts' journal is particularly revealing. When he closes the book, Marcel's first exclamation to himself is, "The Prestige of Literature!" (III, 717). There is something about a written text—its vision, its transparence, its metaphoric quality—that makes it very strong magic. Even against our will it can enter our mental system and exert a lasting influence. Prestige in this sense begins to look little different from snobbery in the social domain. If the patina of heightened existence that hangs over certain lives can be attributed to the secret power of literature, then we can accept the need for a certain portion of artifice to save reality from triviality and platitude. But the converse case that Proust puts forward and that troubles Marcel seems far more devastating. Is there a

[2] Confronted by a similar problem in social relativity theory, Marcel's grandmother has no trouble finding a solution. She discovers that their nice but slightly disreputable neighbor in Combray, Swann, is a close friend of the nephews of the Marquise de Villeparisis, her most aristocratic schoolmate. "Now, this information about Swann had the effect, not of raising him in my grandmother's estimation, but of lowering Mme de Villeparisis" (I, 20).

quality in some people that makes them highly suscepti-
ble to the prestige of literature and yet incapable of
finding its counterpart in their own existence? The
crucial phrase in the last passage quoted, a phrase which
opens in Marcel's line of thought a crevasse falling away
to unknown depths beneath, is "*some infirmity in my
nature*." What precisely is this infirmity that makes
Marcel incapable of taking full account of the very
scenes he has lived through? The answer will tell us
what has made Marcel so prone to the false scents of
society, love, and art.

FROM PLACES TO PEOPLE:
THE "INFIRMITY IN MY NATURE"

During the extended nocturnal musings at the start of
the *Search*, the voice of Proust's Narrator first gathers
strength and identity in a kaleidoscopic description of
bedrooms. He is trying to orient himself, to establish
where he is. Wallace Stevens in his "Adagia" could have
been speaking for Proust: "Life is an affair of people not
of places. But for me life is an affair of places and that
is the trouble." Proust's universe hangs together at the
start more substantially by places than by people, who
are forever disappearing behind new incarnations of
themselves. Each important place takes shape as a
vividly experienced and basically stable association of
light effects, smells, tastes, sounds, history, habitual
behavior patterns, and predictable deviations. Combray
forms a "closed society" (I, 110) with its own laws and
legends. Marcel comes to rely on a similar ritual of
familiar place when he plays in the Champs-Elysées
gardens in Paris. Balbec also stands for a reassuring stability of life. When Marcel returns for his second visit to
this alluring seaside resort, only his outlook on things
has changed. Balbec with its familiar landmarks and
leisurely life seems motionless in time. The early vol-

umes of *Search* depict in convincing detail what Proust
states bluntly in *Jean Santeuil*.

> Places are people, but people who do not change and
> whom we often see again after a long time in wonder-
> ment that we have not remained the same (*JS*, 534).

One can rely on places, above all on landscapes like
Combray and Balbec where man's handiwork blends
with nature.

But as time goes on Marcel loses this security. Paris
apartments and fashionable salons replace countryside
and landscape. These city interiors frame not the dur-
able objects of nature but the inscrutable metamorphoses of men. Even the attractions of Balbec fall victim
to this movement. After a summer full of visits to sites in
the area, Marcel realizes that the exotic local place names
have slowly been "humanized" (II, 1098). He decides to
leave this "much too social valley" (II, 1112). When his
special sensibility to landscape has withered away, only
Venice, still unvisited and unknown, seems to hold out
the power to move him.

The last exterior in the *Search* comes only a few pages
before the last Guermantes reception. Marcel's train
stops in the countryside next to a line of obliquely lit
trees. A sensitized reader will at this point see several
hovering images—the half-lit tower of the Combray
church, the trees the Narrator reflects on in the Bois,
the three trees from which Marcel receives mysterious
signals in Hudimesnil near Balbec (I, 64, 423, 717). But
not Marcel. His light has gone out.

> "Trees," I thought, "there's nothing more you can say
> to me, my chilly heart can no longer hear you. Yet
> here I am in the very lap of nature. Well, I feel only
> indifference and boredom when my eyes follow the
> line that separates your illuminated forehead from
> your shadowy trunk. If I could never before fully

believe myself a poet, I now *know* that I am *not* one"
(III, 855).

Landscape serves no longer, even in retrospect. During
the novel's long meandering, the collection of vivid
scenes which Marcel formerly possessed and which he
could more or less at will slide into his interior stereo-
scope has been subordinated to the characters and absorbed by them. Albertine, an unknowable mixture of
innocence and vice, takes shape out of the exotic topography of Balbec and then displaces it. The richly colored
landscapes of Combray and Balbec fade into the background as the cast of characters moves forward. People
have taken over from places.

This large-scale shift from place to person as the
focus of the narrative provides the background for Marcel's long dedication to society, love, and art. Though
these pursuits may not bring him the rewards he hopes
for, they do seem to lead him out of childhood and toward maturity. Haltingly, he begins to make his way in
the world outside the family unit. Yet Marcel has the
desperate feeling that life is escaping him precisely
when he can for the first time find friends and protectors
and lovers. What has gone wrong? We are dealing again,
I believe, with a quirk of mind that begins very early in
the story as a kind of contrariness, of perverseness in a
spoiled boy.

As a child in Combray, Marcel goes to Machiavellian
lengths to lure his mother up to his bedroom to say
goodnight when she should be downstairs attending to
her guests. The scene is justly celebrated, for it sets the
novel in motion and anticipates many themes to be
developed later. The close of the incident brings its most
revealing moment. When finally his mother does come,
Marcel's father indulgently persuades her to spend the
night in Marcel's room and read him to sleep—thus compromising her principles and her authority. Marcel cannot cope with so great success and inwardly reverses

himself. "If I had dared to now, I would have said to maman: 'No, I don't really want you to, don't sleep here with me' " (I, 38). Her capitulation unmans him.

From this seed will grow a vine of constrictive experience, a vertible tree of forbidden knowledge. In a letter to the Princesse Bibesco, Proust generalized the same reaction. "A sensation, no matter how disinterested it may be, a perfume, or an insight, if they are present, are still too much in my power to make me happy." Steadily and disturbingly, the novel develops this mental set: it is the same "infirmity in my nature" that troubles Marcel when he reads the Goncourts' journal. Toward the end of the evening when he dines for the first time with the Duc and Duchesse de Guermantes, Marcel tries to take stock of his disappointment. I have described how his entry into this most elegant and inaccessible layer of society fails to meet expectations. He finds the explanation not in the other people but *in himself*.

> Several times already I had wanted to leave, and, more than for any other reason, because of the insignificance which my presence imposed on the party. . . . At least my departure would allow the guests, once rid of the interloper, to form a closed group. They would be able to begin the celebration of the mysteries (II, 543–42 . . .).

Because this is still a young dilettante among the dowagers, we might easily laugh off such a moment as something like a failure in social depth perception. It should all straighten out as Marcel gains experience and confidence. Yet he and we remain apprehensive. Even Swann fell victim to this vision of his own presence blighting reality. The part of Odette which he longs above all to know is her "real life as it was when he wasn't there" (I, 299). Marcel feels the same way toward Albertine, and could barely bring himself to kiss her when available.

It is this clouding of the mind at the moment of achieving what it most desires, this "infirmity in my nature," that I call Proust's complaint. He was not the first to discover it, of course. He did not even give it a consistent name. But more than any other writer, Proust explored this distressing perverseness that dogs the most enterprising activities of the human mind and seems to deprive it of satisfaction. One finds, knit tightly into the comedy of the *Search*, a long lament of self-deprecation.

SOUL ERROR

Throughout the seventeenth and eighteenth centuries, in England and on the Continent, the psychological investigations of men's motives concentrated on the theme of pride and the search for fame. The French rolled the two together into the term, *la gloire*. It haunts the work of La Rochefoucauld and La Bruyère, of Corneille and Racine. Milton knew that "Fame is the spur. . ." (*Lycidas*) yet proceeded to condemn it in all its forms except the divine. When Voltaire, Hume, and Kant picked up the theme in an age less concerned with a Christian God, they treated the desire for esteem in the eyes of others as a socially beneficial infirmity. This powerful doctrine accepts human vanity or pride as the necessary engine of culture and as the source of the fair edifices of civilization. The current still runs strong in the nineteenth-century novels of Stendhal and Balzac, who were absorbed by the myth of the young adventurer out to make his mark in the world.

Against this background of *gloire*, Marcel's "infirmity in my nature" looks ludicrous. He hopes for success and fame; what holds him back? Why is he such a miserable hero? Considering his accomplishments, why does he feel this way? The answer is confounding. Marcel cannot win; not because he lacks talent or looks, but *simply because he is Marcel*. His very presence discredits, in his own eyes, whatever he does. After the most elaborate

efforts, he attains goals that turn out to be valueless—
precisely because he has reached them. When he kisses
Albertine, he confronts ten Albertines, no one of whom
he desires. The Guermantes don't live up to expectation.
By a fatality that lodges in his bones or his name or his
being, Marcel carries a pall wherever he goes.

The pattern is endlessly repeated. Having heard from
Swann about the beauties of the Balbec church, Marcel
visits it before going on to the hotel and the beach. When
he finds the church surrounded by ugly buildings and
"reduced to its own stone countenance," he is bitterly
disappointed. The precious work of art is overwhelmed
by the proximity of a pastry shop and the branch office
of a bank. The promise of its name crumbles under "the
tyranny of the Particular" (I, 660). Later, near Balbec,
Marcel accosts a pretty fishergirl in such a boasting
manner that he knows she will remember him. For a
moment he desires her and forces himself on her
attention.

> And that capturing of her mind, that immaterial
> possession, was enough to strip her of mystery as
> fully as physical possession (I, 717).

In his success is his failure.

Does the flaw that causes this condition lodge entirely
in Marcel's sensibility, as is implied by the phase "infirmity in my nature"? Before accepting this verdict, we
would do well to look again at the pattern of events that
surrounds Marcel. One persuasive answer to the question
would be that the real flaw is not simply a character
trait but arises out of the relation between subjective
and objective. We already have the terms available.
When the intermittence of our natures meets the per-
verse timing of events, the result is a puzzling disarray.

> Our desires interfere constantly with one another,
> and, in the confusion of our existence, it is rare that
> happiness coincides with the desire that clamored for
> it (I, 489).

The two series will not mesh. Odette falls passionately in love with Swann when she first meets him, yet those feelings fade before his infatuation begins. This explanation of Proust's complaint by intermittence and timing appeals to an unexamined fatalism. It posits that we must simply accept the fact that his (our) condition springs from an inevitable semicomic discrepancy between subjective desire and objective reality.

I believe we can go further in seeking the origins of Marcel's habit of self-doubt. It seems fully appropriate that one of the keenest descriptions of this temper was written four centuries ago by Montaigne. In the first version of the essay "On Presumption," he is speaking of the outward signs of vainglory. That vice arises, he says, either out of too high an opinion of oneself or out of too low an opinion of others. Then suddenly—at least it feels sudden when you come upon the passage Montaigne inserted many years later into the original text—he shifts his ground. Now it is a sixty-year-old man speaking a deeper truth than he knew at forty.

> I feel oppressed by *an error of mind* which offends me both as unjust and even more as annoying. I try to correct it, but I cannot root it out. *It is that I attach too little value to things I possess, just because I possess them; and overvalue anything strange, absent, and not mine.* This frame of mind extends very far. As the prerogative of authority leads men to regard their wives with monstrous disdain, and sometimes their children, so too am I afflicted. Whatever I am responsible for can never, as I see things, meet the competition. To an even greater degree, any desire for advancment and improvement clouds my judgment and closes off the path to satisfaction, just as mastery in itself breeds scorn of whatever one holds in one's power. Exotic societies, customs, and languages attract me, and I realize that the dignity of Latin impresses me more than it should, just as it does children and common folk. My neighbor's house, the way he runs his affairs, his horse, though no

better than my own, are all worth more than mine
precisely because they are not mine [italics added].

In this passage Montaigne is right on pitch, perfectly in
tune with himself and with that human condition we
share with him. Here is the subtlest and most far-
reaching fault of all. It strikes at our very sense of
reality. *Soul error*[3] is the incapacity to give full value or
status to one's own life and experience. This quiet
southern gentleman, former mayor of Bordeaux and
companion of kings, retired to a tower and devoted his
life to writing about himself. One would expect to find
the most self-satisfied, the least self-deprecating of men.
Yet it is he who tells us in the same essay: ". . . it would
be difficult for any man to have a poorer opinion of
himself."

Here then is the "tyranny of the Particular"—but directed by Montaigne back at ourselves. For we are our
own principal particular. We find ourselves and all that
belongs to us very hard to live with. Soul error: Proust,
the Narrator, and Marcel wrestle with it. The only escape
Proust suggests is to seek an impossible perfection (II,
46) or the inaccessible (III, 384). That way one keeps
one's face averted from the real. But in his writing, soul
error is never far away. In one of the early texts published in *Pleasures and Days*, Proust writes of a ten-year-
old boy who tries to kill himself out of love for an older
girl. Has she scorned him? No. "He felt disappointment
every time he saw the sovereign of his dreams; but as
soon as she had gone, his fertile imagination gave back

---

[3] Montaigne's phrase is *une erreur d'âme*. Florio and J. M.
Cohen translate it as "an error of the mind." Donald Frame
tries "an error of my soul." Montaigne does not use the
genitive, which would be *erreur de l'âme*. The French syntax
implies substance, essential composition, as in the forms
crise de nerfs, *état d'esprit*, or even *chemin de fer*. My own
translation proposes "an error of mind." However, English
and American usage of both sixteenth and twentieth centuries offers a tighter version than any of the above: *soul
error*.

to the absent girl all her charms and he wanted to see her again" (*JS*, 111). At the restaurant in Rivebelle, the elegant customers act as compulsively as Marcel. ". . . at each table the diners had eyes only for the tables at which they were not seated. . ." (I, 811). When Mme de Stermaria accepts Marcel's invitation to an intimate dinner in the Bois, he finds he would prefer to have the evening free to try to see other women (II, 391). *Whatever bends to our desire disqualifies itself by becoming a part of ourselves.* Whence the flat statement from the Narrator during Marcel's agonizing separation from Albertine: "Man is the being who cannot get out of himself, who knows others only in himself, and, if he denies it, lies" (III, 450).

Once it has attacked, there is no escape from the worm of self-contempt. For Marcel, only one set of experiences remains immune: the closed world of Combray, where place, family, and nature congeal into a vision barely shadowed by advance warnings of dangers to come. For a precious moment Marcel was content to be himself. Childhood provides the standard of things as they were before the worm attacked them.

Still it is too imprecise simply to say that soul error arises from a loss of the unified world of childhood. For just how does it come about that reality and appearance part company? Combray exists retroactively for Marcel as a benevolent but inflexible routine, a *train-train*, within which he discovers for himself the catastrophic factor of time. His goodnight kiss is withheld when he needs it and granted when he wants it no longer. That incident breaks the spell of Combray and infects his experience with the decay of time. Marcel has to face what Proust had already expressed in *Pleasures and Days*. "No sooner has an anticipated future become the present than it loses its charms." Temporality introduces "an incurable imperfection into the very essence of the present" (*JS*, 139). When Marcel gets high on wine while dining with Saint-Loup at Rivebelle, the euphoria or "pure phenomenism" (I, 816) he feels, approximates a return to total immersion in the present. Exalted tipsiness annuls the discovery of time. While tingling with wine he could forget everything but the intensity of the moment. However, this state represents not a conquest of temporality but a surrender to it.

The "imperfection" in reality imposed by time is accompanied, Proust shows us, by an increased (but far from compensating) power of the imagination. It is the principal internal organ of desire. When Proust describes the young boy in love with a girl who disappoints him every time he sees her, he attributes the boy's malady to his precocious imagination (*JS*, 111). Albertine's "mystery, which she had for me on the beach before I knew her" (II, 363) is a pure product of the imagination. And its functioning observes a precise relation to presence and absence. "Man of imagination, you can find enjoyment only through regret or expectation, that is, in the past or in the future" (*JS*, 54). Twenty years later, Proust was even more categorical. He sees "an inevitable law which arranges things so that one can imagine only what is absent" (III, 872). We may have learned why. Thwarted by intermittence and the warped timing of experience, the imagination falls victim to soul error and seeks its object forever elsewhere.

THE PARADOX OF CONSCIOUSNESS

All literature may aspire to the condition of the proverb. Proverbs appear to record a state of things so compact and definitive that we can tuck them away and forget them until their turn comes around again—as it always does. The one dimension they lack is the dramatic. On the other hand, the manner in which Proust (like Montaigne) devoted the last fifteen years of his life to a single monumental work, and with such intensity as to signify that the work *took* his life, has a clear dramatic ring that echoes through the *Search*. Nevertheless, *roman-fleuve* and proverb are by no means irreconcilable modes. Raymond Radiguet, a sage at seventeen when he wrote *The Devil in the Flesh*, spoke cannily of literature as a means to *"déniaiser les lieux communs."*[4] There is much to be learned from the wisdom worn into the folds of language itself. It is not surprising to find a pair of matched proverbs in English to elucidate Proust's complaint. A comparable pair exists in many languages.

The romantic version has a strong ironic counter-thrust, and its pastoral metaphor makes it suitable for hymns and popular songs: *the grass is greener on the other side of the fence—or hill*. The realist version is terser and has an edge of cynicism: *familiarity breeds contempt*. Once heard, they remain. Of all the major characters in the *Search*, Françoise has the most humble origins, yet she outlasts all the others, including the Narrator himself. Similarly, Proust finally leads us to proverbs, sturdy little shrines in the landscape of human experience. They cannot replace his novel, but they may well outlast it. And they also caution us not to dismiss or underrate the state of mind I have been describing. Through Marcel, Proust places soul error at the crossroads of his novel and develops it as a powerful metamorphosis of the flaw we knew first as Greek hubris and Christian pride. The *Search* makes a man of its maxims by gradually laying bare several closely joined aspects of Proust's complaint. I shall distinguish here between three: the pathos of thought, the pathos of self, and the paradox of individual consciousness.

If, as I wrote earlier, Proust shows temporality and the imagination working together to infect the present with unreality, then we confront an essential character of thought: our incapacity to conceive and assimilate

[4]Here lies a translator's nemesis—or fortune. "To give meaning to the commonplace." "To teach clichés the facts of life." "To make a man of a maxim."

what immediately confronts us. The pathos of thought begins with the realization that thinking always operates at a distance, at one remove. The subjective mind cannot fuse with objective reality. All the examples I have been giving outline an attitude very close to the one Rousseau has Julie express in *La Nouvelle Héloïse*: "In this world the realm of fantasy or of fiction [*chimères*] is the only one worth living in, and the emptiness of human things is so great that, except for Being itself, nothing is beautiful but what does not exist." This is an extreme form of our yearning for elsewhere, of our squirming against being where we are. The mood creates around it an aura of anxiety, emanating from the knowledge that our very presence anywhere is a form of intrusion. An added consciousness interferes with the goings-on. Whence Marcel's eternal desire to spy on people, to be simultaneously present and absent.

As is often the case when he wants to give particular emphasis to his point, Proust finds a scientific comparison for the pathos of thought. Marcel is reading, hidden in a little shelter or recess in the depths of the garden.

> And didn't my thinking resemble yet another recess in the depths of which I felt caught, even if I wanted to look out at things around me? When I saw an external object, my consciousness that I was seeing it remained between me and it, outlining it with a narrow mental border that prevented me from ever touching its substance directly; in some way the object volatilized before I could make contact, just as an incandescent body approaching something moist never reaches moisture because of the zone of evaporation that always precedes such a body (I, 84).

Mere awareness volatilizes what it seeks and hampers its own functioning. The most reflective of us are endowed with the antithesis of Midas's touch; it turns the things we want, or want to know, into dross. In the sphere of love, Stendhal gave a name to the common and distressing weakness that renders a man physically incapable of doing precisely what he most desires to do. *Fiasco*, in any language, can no longer mean just a jug of wine. But Proust felt fiasco writ very large. He comprehended a greater disaster: not only that familiarity breeds contempt, but also that merely to think something diminishes the dimensions of its reality. Imagining impedes realization. It is impossible to be present at the coronation of one's own happiness: recall Marcel kissing Albertine. No wonder Proust spent his years writing his way out from under the burden of being alive, and of being aware of being alive.

For our culture, Faust represents this pathos of thought. There is no happiness or repose for his overactive mind, only for the new community of citizens he creates by draining swamplands. In this perspective of restlessness, Faust's lot looks very similar to that of Don Juan, who embodies the pathos of self. Both their stories arise from a perception of life as flawed. We are born into dissatisfaction with our estate. Society constrains us to limit our behavior to patterns assigned not only by our public role but also by expectations of consistent character. We are usually barred from acting out all our conflicting feelings and responses. But even without social conventions, our behavior displays the features of what I have referred to as intermittence. It is beyond our power as humans to be all of ourselves at once. Our finite capacity for existence makes our character successive, dependent on time to reveal itself in any depth. Impatient with this inability to assume ourselves entire at any point in time, we react by yearning to enter into or become someone else, to escape the limits of our own body and being. What Marcel shares with Don Juan is a gnawing dissatisfaction with himself, compounded by the feeling that he cannot fully possess the persons he desires. The urge for self-transcendence burns a hole in our being without ever attaining its goal: true otherness.

Proust's Narrator comes back many times to the dynamics of this process. He describes it in fact as a consequence of the pathos of thought. The "narrow mental border" that isolates us from the world around us has an effect on our sense of self.

> For even if we have the sensation of being always enveloped in, and surrounded by our own soul, still it does not seem a fixed and immovable prison; rather we seem to be borne away with it, and perpetually struggling to break out of it into the world, with constant discouragement when we hear endlessly, all around us, that unvarying sound which is not an echo from without, but the resonance of a vibration from within (I, 86).

We are stuck inside ourselves. Two thousand pages later the narrator has still not found his way out. He says that even a pair of wings and a new respiratory system that would allow us to survive on Mars would not take us out of ourselves so long as we had to use the same senses and our own consciousness. The conclusion has a desperate ring.

> The only true voyage, the only Fountain of Youth, would be found not in traveling to strange lands but in having different eyes, in seeing the universe with the eyes of another person, of a hundred others, and seeing the hundred universes each of them sees, which each of them is (III, 258).

The desire of the imagination to outstrip the self is as urgent as it is hopeless. Marcel moves through the world in a kind of tightly enclosed, yet partially transparent gondola. This confinement, and the intense spiritual and even physical activity it provokes, is what I mean by pathos of self.

My third gloss on the proverb version of Proust's complaint departs only slightly from the other two. Yet it introduces a now familiar concept that may illuminate a key segment of Proust's thinking. It also displays the way our universe seems to fold back on itself when one reaches one of its remotest corners.

When modern physicists began to explore elementary particles of matter, they realized that certain things were happening which ran counter to accepted laws or regularities of determinism. In order to explain these events, Werner Heisenberg formulated the indeterminacy principle. Fully developed, that principle combines two very different sets of phenomena, on an atomic order of magnitude. First, submicroscopic events like the radiation of a specific particle of radium cannot be predicted. Even statistical probabilities can be calculated only for significant quantities of particles. Single particles appear independent of traditional determinism. Second, the impress of energy required for accurate observation (i.e., some equivalent of light on the subject) is in itself sufficient to modify the event under observation. Thus, at the level of atomic magnitudes, we can neither predict nor observe with accuracy.

I would suggest that probers of the human consciousness like Proust reveal a comparable indeterminacy principle that describes processes on the level of individual thought. The disruptions and irregularities of one man's thinking cannot be predicted. General statements about a statistically significant sample of individuals are another matter. Furthermore, observation (including self-observation) close enough to penetrate inside a person's consciousness provokes a disturbance sufficient to vitiate the observation. (See Proust's second answer to the question "Your ideal of earthly happiness?" cited above, p. 12.) Mere witnessing modifies the course of human actions. Many authors, from Rousseau to Dostoevski, lead us toward an awareness of this double bind. Proust's exploration of the psyche makes it almost impossible to deny the validity of something like an indeterminacy principle at the level of individual thought. This paradox of consciousness fetters us to a modicum of ignorance about what we might otherwise expect to know best: our kind and ourselves. Proust is describing the condition in the passage quoted on page 101, particularly with the word *liséré*—border, or outline, or margin. He uses it one other time, near the end of the novel, unforgetful of the earlier passage, and now making perfectly clear the double thrust he means to give the word. Uncertainty inheres both in things (contingencies) and in consciousness (perception).

> For there exists between us and all beings a border [*liséré*] of contingencies, just as I had understood while reading in Combray that there is a border of perception which prevents perfect contact between reality and the mind (III, 975).

The origins of Proust's complaint reach back to this dark region of mind where, alone, we face the problems of reality and communication.

Marcel's efforts to break out of these confinements of self have already been described in terms of social climbing, love, and art. Those three false leads throw him back even more desperately on himself. He is left with few resources, one of which we hear about very early in the *Search*. "Habit! that skillful arranger" (I, 8). As the novel opens, and repeatedly thereafter, Marcel imagines his life as a series of bedrooms to which he becomes accustomed. Their familiarity as places sustains his identity as a person. The accomplishment of life's major tasks, the Narrator tells us, relies more on habit than on "momentary transports" (I, 93). It also provides our security, for habit "drapes over things the guise of familiarity rather than showing their true being, which would frighten us" (II, 764). Marcel's psychic survival under the curse of soul error depends on the defense of habit which "regulates the economy of our nervous system" (III, 918); but it is survival on a low level of being and happiness. Marcel clings to routine and blesses the comforts of the familiar even while another part of his mind knows that he is missing the truths and satisfactions he seeks from life.

The Narrator's steady presence in the text embodies a different response to the paradoxes of consciousness and self. (Marcel gradually approaches this attitude, which is more flexible and rewarding than his reliance on habit.) It is the opposite of intolerance and defiance of those inward failings in an effort to overcome them. In seeking to transcend their humanity, Faust and Don Juan aimed at glory and immortality as ambitiously as any Pharaoh or world conqueror. Yet their aspirations to divinity by means of surpassing the human condition contain the seeds of a tragic fall.

What Proust portrays in the Narrator is a more direct and modest attitude toward mortality. The descriptions of consciousness as rarely whole and beset by impossible desires for otherness show how deeply flawed life is. The *Search* as a whole seeks not to transcend that condition but to encompass it. *Intermittence* is the guiding principle. The action transpires by lingering seasons and stages. The book becomes oceanic in scale in order to contain the changing weathers and tides and crosscurrents of a long voyage. There is no synthesis, no higher calculus to which these manifold cycles can be reduced. Intermittence describes a sequence of variations without prescribing their course or regularity. Correspondingly, since we cannot assume all parts of our character at a particular moment or grasp the full significance of our experience as it occurs, it is wise to recognize and tolerate this temporal aspect of our humanity. To oppose it is folly. As a basic insight into the pulse of life, intermittence means that Marcel gradually learns to bear and reflect upon fluctuations of self and experience through periods of long duration. He speaks occasionally and misleadingly of general laws, but he lives with, and through, vividly alternating particulars. The same applies to the reader following the text. In letters to two prospective editors in 1912, Proust proposed a general title for his unpublished novel: "Intermittences of Heart." He would have done well to keep it.

Without shuffling off the tribulations of soul error, we have reached a universe of sympathy and understanding far removed from the fanaticism that propels tragedy. In this universe where everything connects, the next observation should seem natural. "The infirmity in my nature" that convinces Marcel he is always a wet blanket, and "the narrow mental border" that intervenes between his subjective perceptions and the objective world he longs to reach, are extensions of the comic vision. Consciousness itself partakes of the comic. Marcel, watched patiently by the Narrator, stumbles over his mortality both when he ventures out into society or tries to kiss a girl and also in the innermost workings of his thought. Intermittence links the conflicting segments of his life through age and cumulative experience without invoking a transcendent vision out of time. Fully understood as part of our lot, Proust's complaint leads not to despair but to a gentle smile at the vagaries of men and at the time it takes them to recognize themselves for what they are.

Spinning a Yarn

V

Many years ago a New York publishing firm issued a collection of orchestral scores with arrows prominently overprinted to designate the instrument carrying the melody. Presumably this was the line one should follow. Intelligent musicians immediately criticized these "Arrow Guides" as a travesty of music. One must listen to the entire texture of relationships, they insisted, and not just pick out a melody.

What forms and directs Proust's work is not any one strand that can be singled out and followed through the entire fabric. It is rather a sustained mental movement producing tension, comparable to the spinning of many fibers into thread or yarn, into the clothes on our backs, into the very struts and cordage of civilized life. The thickest rope is worthless unless its filaments have been twisted tight. Friction sustains us. The strength of Proust's work resides in the turning and tossing of a mind engaged with many recurring themes. That inexhaustible activity did finally weave a fabric sturdy enough to intertwine the comic and soul error. In fact, I have emphasized those two strands of the *Search* because they reveal the perpetual motion of Proust's sensibility. He never stopped spinning, and pulling the strands snugly together. I have passed over several elements whose significance in his work is widely and properly recognized. The time has come to deal with them.

A CASE HISTORY

Because of its constant preoccupation with states of mind and hidden motivation, the *Search* seems to qualify as an exhaustive psychoanalytic case history. Of course, Proust did not discover the unconscious and the influence of long-forgotten or suppressed events by reading Freud. Furthermore the novel does not simply record Proust's own case (see above, pages 20–21).

Beginning with recognizable symptoms of anxiety, the Narrator of the *Search* carries his explorations back into the past until he locates the magnetized and luminous event that lies at the source of everything. Then the case history moves forward through successive revelations that grow in scale and detail until they seem to lay bare the patient's life. "Analysis" is constantly going on, probing toward the functioning of the psyche. Can we distinguish patient from analyst in this narrative? The two persons of the drama are not separated here by professional competence, signified by the paying of a fee; they are separated by age and experience, as signified by various overt and covert signals in the narrative voice. The *Search* records the achingly sustained self-analysis of a fictional character projected into the double role of Marcel and the Narrator. Both of them contribute passages of deep analysis that sometimes seem to bring the action to a full stop. Yet it always moves on. The *Search* remains fundamentally a story—a temporal, linear narrative in which the reader feels a pressure of events propelling him from a beginning toward an end. The general movement is a growing up and a growing old.

Marcel's specific case circles around the question of resolution, of will power. When the lens of the narrative comes into focus in the opening pages, it fixes on Marcel's first self-affirmation as a child. "I had just made the resolution not to try to go to sleep without seeing maman again, and to kiss her whatever happened" (I, 32). This resolution leads to a double abdication: his mother's, when she indulges his whim; and his own, when he cannot confess that he doesn't really want her to spend the night in his room after all. The story begins with a compound failure. Near the end of the novel, Marcel goes through an analogous sequence, but in reverse order and at another level. Arriving at the Prince de Guermantes's reception, he begins his long meditation on literature as a vocation. Here Marcel explicitly abstains from any rash resolution. "In the middle of all this I realized that, in the work of art I felt ready to undertake without having consciously resolved to do so, there would be great difficulties" (III, 870). His skepticism lasts through one hundred fifty pages of soliloquizing and anguished socializing until he suddenly confronts the incarnation of his past and of lived time in the form of Mlle de Saint-Loup. This "goad" to his will tells him that it is time at last to begin writing the book that will show his life as worth living (III, 1032). And he does begin. Skepticism gives way to dedication. The moral strength that abandoned him and his mother in the opening pages comes back here at the end and allows him to record its case history.

Between these two events lies a lifetime full of personal experience and suffering. Marcel has to learn all his lessons for himself. But how does he survive the voyage? And why does the action seem to face the past

so steadily as it moves forward in time? The earliest
events of the story in Combray are bathed in a feeling of
reverence that the accompanying comedy does not
diminish. Aunt Léonie's house has as magical and symbolic an existence as the village church. Is there an
authority that ties us to our childhood more than to any
other period? On this point the novel is clear: *faith*
makes the difference. As children, *we believe in the
world around us* as we never shall again. The Narrator
states the case in the closing pages of "Combray."

> But I regard the Méséglise and the Guermantes's ways
> primarily as the deepest layer of my mental soil, as
> firm ground on which I can still stand. It is because
> I used to believe[1] in things and in beings while I
> walked along these two paths that the things and the
> beings they made known to me are the only ones that
> I still take seriously, the only ones that bring me joy.
> Whether it is because the faith which creates has
> ceased to exist in me, or because reality will take
> shape in the memory alone, the flowers that people
> show me nowadays for the first time never seem to be
> true flowers (I, 184).

In spite of strong family tensions and dark forebodings,
Combray possesses the one essential quality that transforms it into Eden for Marcel. The congruence of his
faith in desired things with the real presence of those
things close to him produces a wholeness of experience
that stays in his memory. It provides the eternal standard of a world not yet sundered by soul error. Once upon
a time we were all believers in the completeness of our
own existence. Faith in one's own experience: do we
need any further description of Eden? As an old man at
the end of the novel, Marcel imagines how a young stu-
dent, like himself many years before, might still be

[1] Unfortunately, Moncrieff here mistranslates *croyais* as
"think of" instead of "believe in" and obscures a crucial
point.

enchanted by the Guermantes mansion on the Avenue du Bois. "It is because he is still in the age of belief, which I had left far behind" (III, 858).[2]

Combray means a time of life, an age of belief. It represents not only wholeness of experience but also the domain where the child remains in close proximity to unmediated sensation in the form of impressions. The narrative uses the two ways as a topographical scheme (almost like the mnemonic devices actors once relied on to learn their lines) of sorting out impressions into two contrasting sets. We later learn how inadequate the two ways really are as an organizing principle. They stand firm because Marcel once believed in them. On the other hand, his first impressions, in which he loses faith all too soon as he grows up, turn out to be accurate. Twice toward the end of the novel the Narrator points out that Marcel's first impressions of Gilberte and Albertine as precocious and lascivious young hussies were right after all (III, 609, 694). Proust was not so misguided as to believe we can revert to childhood or naïve sensation. Yet his literary imagination and stylistic power were bent on capturing the reverence of childhood experience. The important thing about the *Search* as a case history is not its presentation of Proust's neuroses or coenesthesia or homosexuality. It is the way Marcel keeps the faith in spite of terrible reverses and finally finds the resolve to create a present for himself that encompasses the past. Living is nine-tenths endurance.

TWO DISPUTES

For many years the length and title of the *Search*, its depiction of age, and its emphasis on memory convinced

[2] The German writer Hugo Ball also discovered the meaning of this kind of belief. In his deeply meditative journal, *Die Flucht aus der Zeit*, he describes Adam as the man "who believed in his surroundings."

most readers that the book's essential subject is time and
temporality. It conveys above all a sense of time deeply
penetrated and linked back to itself in wide loops of
recall and recognition. This approach lends weight to the
order and pacing of events and endorses the conception
of a story as basically linear, or perhaps circular, like
time itself. In recent years, however, a number of critics
have taken up their cudgels to make the opposite case.
When one has finished the novel, they contend, when
one can hold its parts together in the mind, its true
character reveals itself as that of a single whole which
stands free of temporal order and lies spread out before
us in space, like a painting.

In this case, as usual, Proust speaks eloquently on
both sides of the questions. In the "interview" he supplied in 1913 for the journalist Elie-Joseph Bois (the text
appears in the Appendix, pages 167–172), Proust justi-
fies the still undivulged length of his novel by saying it
will portray "psychology in time. It is this invisible substance of time that I have tried to isolate." And when the
last volume appeared fifteen years later, he insisted all
over again that the book was cast in "the form of Time"
(III, 145; *cf.* III, 1149). The opening sentence of the
entire work as well as its title indicate a constant co-
habitation with time. The case would seem clear from
the start. Yet, particularly in the decisive closing pages,
Proust uses figures that describe a reaction against temporality. In the sentences that immediately precede the
moment when the tide of the action turns and Marcel
steps on the uneven paving stones, he complains that
living to be a hundred would bring no reward. For it
would mean nothing more than "successive extensions
of a life laid out along one line" (III, 866). Images of
height and architectural construction in the final pages
seem to imply a new perspective. Proust had formulated
the shift most tersely when speaking of architecture in
an early draft of the novel: "Time has assumed the form

of space" (*CSB*, 285). A building in different styles displays time as simultaneous. To what degree does the *Search* aspire to the condition of architecture?

Now time poses the crucial problem of how we know things, particularly how we know people, over a period of days or years. Proust never wandered far from this problem. Exasperated by his uncertainty over Albertine's and Andrée's unstable feelings toward him, Marcel tells himself in desperation that the only way to find out about their sentiments would be for him to "immobilize" them in order to examine the pattern of their behavior. But he could do so only by ceasing to desire them, for desire provokes change. Without desire he would no longer care about their feelings. The passage concludes glumly: "the stability we attribute to natural things is purely fictive and serves the convenience of language" (III, 64–65). Immobility may permit knowledge, but it arrests life and love. Hence we can never know anyone we love. Such paradoxes of temporality permeate the incidents of the story.

Chronology itself raises parallel problems. Just how far does experience arise from or conform to the temporal order of events? While falling out of love with Gilberte, Marcel finds calendar time utterly meaningless.

> Often (since our life is chronological to so small a degree and inserts so many anachronisms into the sequence of our days) I found myself living a day or two behind myself, going back through stages when I still loved Gilberte (I, 642).

Yet in a later passage about what happens to Saint-Loup and Charlus as they grow older, the Narrator proclaims the opposite dogma: "Everything is a question of chronology" (III, 737*n*).

In the face of these contradictions, and with strong leads from Ortega y Gasset and Raymond Fernandez, two recent critics have taken a categorical position. In an essay called "Spatial Form in Modern Literature"

(1945), Joseph Frank lumps Proust with Pound, Eliot, and Joyce as overdeveloped Imagists. They all incorporate in lengthy works Pound's original definition of an Image: to present "an intellectual and emotional complex in an instant of time." The length and temporal narrative of the *Search* should not deceive us, Frank argues. "Proust's purpose is only achieved, therefore, when these units of meaning [impressions and views of his characters] are referred to each other reflexively in a moment of time." A moment of time Frank interprets as not time at all but as space. Almost twenty years later the Belgian critic Georges Poulet defended the same thesis at greater length. Proust's narrative "juxtaposes" discontinuous images "exhibited side by side" as in a museum. "Thus time yields to space."[3]

Both these critics have much to say on Proust that is revealing. However, on this major point about time they are as misguided as pre-Darwin (and pre-Lyell) biologists trying to develop a theory of the origin of the species without a huge tract of prehistoric time during which variations and selection could occur. How does a mind achieve this spatialization of time? The events and thoughts of Proust's novel, if they are genuinely spatial in Frank's sense, would have to conform to the principle that binds the units of meaning in Pound's *Cantos*: ". . . while they follow one another in time, their meaning does not depend on this temporal relationship." Poulet argues the same case in more homely terms.

> Intact . . . caught in their frames, the episodes of Proust's novel present themselves in an order which is not temporal since it is anachronous, but which cannot be anything other than spatial, since, like a row of jam pots in the magic cupboards of our childhood, it sets out a series of closed vessels in the caverns of the mind.[4]

[3] *L'Espace proustien*, p. 130.
[4] *Ibid.*, p. 134.

In order to persuade us that the order of events in Marcel's life has no significance, Poulet shows him storing those events in a kind of mental larder, with no temporal sequence. The figure applies fairly well to *Jean Santeuil* or to *Against Sainte-Beuve*. But we are dealing with a linear story which Proust carefully and properly called a *search*. Far more aptly it could be represented as a climb to the top of a mountain. The view from the summit does indeed set out before one an arrangement of the landscape that allows one's gaze to move at will from feature to feature and to take it all in at once. That view is essentially spatial. But it does not and cannot abolish the climb that took one to the summit, and the temporal order of events in that climb. One cannot climb the last hundred feet before the first. Marcel could not have loved Albertine before Gilberte, nor could he have become a writer without the years of discouragement and disillusion that seemed to be leading him in quite another direction. Marcel remains the creature of a temporal order of events that obtains even in retrospect. "Just like the future, it is not all at once but grain by grain that one tastes the past" (III, 531).

But we must go beyond isolated quotations picked shrewdly out of 3000 pages of waiting prose. If a spatial simultaneous vision of the past were Proust's fundamental purpose, then all the early pages would become strictly preparatory and subsidiary. They would in effect drop off, and we would be left with an intense hundred-page essay on the rewards of memory and the nature of literature.[5] Everything I shall have to say about the esthetic attitude and the composition of the *Search* will weigh against this one-sided interpretation.

[5] I believe that Proust had such an expository, nonnarrative plan in mind when he began to work on *Against Sainte-Beuve*. As I have already suggested, the Preface sets down his basic philosophic attitude with only a highly abbreviated version of how he reached it. He abandoned the plan almost as soon as he began writing.

The *Search* affirms *both* perspectives. On one hand, it insists on the lived temporal order of things, which combines individual development with a sense of the gradual modulation of reality itself. On the other hand, it focuses on occasional resurrections revealing a glimpse of the past outside of contingent time and creating patterns so convincing as to be called essences. A mass of evidence, passed over by Frank and Poulet, suggests that the temporal sequence dominates most of the narrative and withdraws conditionally in favor of the spatial arrangement only at the start and again as its end approaches. This close relation between time and space in the novel as a whole parallels the art of description insisted upon by the Narrator (III, 319, 591). True description follows the temporal order of impressions—a kind of innocence reintroduced into experience otherwise encrusted by habit—before accepting a ready-made concept or a word. The interchange never stops. The *Search* creates a predominantly temporal perspective, scored through deeply at crucial moments by arresting spatial insights. The only synthesis resides in the full dimensions of the work itself.

These concerns led Proust to give serious attention to music, an art whose performance is entirely temporal, yet whose form may be spatialized by repetition and memory. In two closely related passages, one toward the beginning and the other toward the end of the novel, Proust describes that double experience. In the first, Marcel is listening to Odette play the piano.

> It was on one of those days that she happened to play for me the part of Vinteuil's sonata that contained the little phrase of which Swann had been so fond. But often, if it is a complicated piece of music to which one is listening for the first time, one listens and hears nothing. . . . That gives rise to the melancholy that clings to the knowledge of such works, as of everything that takes place in time. . . . Since I was able to enjoy the pleasure that this sonata gave me only

in a succession of hearings, I never possessed it in its entirety: it was like life itself. But great works of art are less disappointing than life, for they do not begin by giving us the best of themselves (I, 529–31).

The passage contains a tentative esthetic. The experience of complex music is cumulative, subject to time, never exhaustive. It differs from life in that its greatest rewards come late and not early. The *Search* itself, we realize, observes this rhythm of delayed revelation. The time needed for gradual initiation to a work of art belongs to and forms part of its experience. An instant does not contain it, though art may contain exalted instants.

In the counterpart scene many years later, Marcel discovers in music an even deeper synthesis of temporal and spatial experiences. Albertine is selecting to play for Marcel on the pianola, not familiar works, but new pieces whose shape is still obscure for him. The Narrator distinguishes carefully between two experiences of these unfamiliar pieces. First comes a slowly built-up deposit of successive playings, which he describes as "a volume, produced by the unequal visibility of the different phrases." Later, Marcel can project and immobilize the different parts "on a uniform plane," open to inspection by his intelligence (III, 373). The next sentence tells us not that one aspect is higher or more final than the other but that what brings a reward is the movement between the pathos of temporal experience and the immobility of analytic intelligence.

> [Albertine] did not yet go on to another piece, for, without being really aware of the process taking place inside me, she knew that at the moment when my intelligence had succeeded in dispelling the mystery of a piece, it had almost always, in the course of its ill-fated work, discovered in compensation some profitable reflection (III, 373).

The shift from shadowy time to brightly lit space would be "ill-fated" (*néfaste*), injurious to the sensibility, were it not for the fact that this shift in psychic levels brings a reward in some other realm of the mind.[6] Furthermore, the knowledge wrested by intelligence out of the flux sends Marcel continually back toward temporality and mortality. There is always another piece of music to listen to and understand. After the pinnacles of atemporal vision at the end, Marcel's reward comes in the form of the very down-to-earth discovery that "life was worth living" (III, 1032). Time and space do not try to elbow one another aside in the *Search* in order to dominate the scene. They perform an elaborate and moving saraband that leaves both on stage and in full possession of their powers.

The second dispute that hangs over Proust's work is partially implicit in the first, and it centers on the nature of our mental faculties.

I sometimes feel that the long essay on memory, time, and art in the closing pages of the *Search* does a disservice to the understanding of the novel. Proust's discursive, almost magisterial tone in those pages leads one to expect a final declaration that will weave back together all the raveled ends and resolve all contradictions. Critics with a hypothesis to support will often pick most of their quotations from this section, as if it were more probative than any other. Proust gives them every reason to act this way. Yet the lesson of unreason many critics have read into these pages conflicts with the lucidity and logical sequence of its style.

[6] If I understand Proust properly here, he is taking a step beyond the approach to art proposed by Ernst Kris in *Psychoanalytic Explorations in Art* (New York, 1962). Kris proposes that esthetic experience entails a process by which we find pleasurable in itself a shift in mental energy, a change in psychic level, if kept under control of the ego. Proust seems to believe that the mental shift from temporal hearing to simultaneous understanding of music carries value not as an ascent to a higher level, and not as a pleasure in itself, but because it usually released other mental insights. This undeveloped idea hints at a further argument against the idolatry of art, against art for art's sake.

Beginning with the earliest reviewers, there has been wide agreement that Proust's portrait of the writer in the *Search* (and, by implication, of himself) presents a man passively responding to experience. Georges Bataille refers to "the rigor with which he reduces the object of his search to *involuntary* discovery." Gilles Deleuze devotes his entire last chapter to Proust's thought as a form of abdication of will. "The great theme of *Time Regained* is that the search for truth is the characteristic adventure of the involuntary. Thought is nothing without something which forces and does violence to it." Most of these critics hunt out the Narrator's commentary on sudden memories near the start of the final commentary.

> I had not gone out looking for the two uneven paving stones in the courtyard which I had stepped on. But precisely the fortuitous and inevitable way in which the sensation had come about determined the truth of the past it resurrected and of the images it set in motion (III, 879).

Fortuitous and *inevitable*. Choice, will, and deliberation thus appear to have no role to play in provoking a reminiscence. Beginning with the Madeleine sequence at the start of the novel, the Narrator insists on the involuntary nature of such experiences.

Do the original impressions, which provide the content of the reminiscences, conform to this pattern? Are they also untainted by any exercise of will? In its full freshness an impression appears simply to impinge on Marcel's senses as an immediate and vivid whole. He never wills an impression, though his mental tonus clearly affects his receptivity. However, it is significant that Marcel does not record as major events—and often omits them altogether—the initial impressions that surge back later in the major reminiscences. He was mildly aware of the starched napkin at Balbec, of the whistles of pleasure boats, and of George Sand's novel *François le Champi*; but none of them struck him as anything more

than an incidental part of the moment. He barely registered any taste or odor of the tea-soaked Madeleine when
his Aunt Léonie offered him a piece (I, 52). It merely
formed a fragment of her world. He apparently took so
little notice of the uneven paving stones in the baptistery
of Saint Mark in Venice that he didn't even mention
them at the time. When he saw the line of trees from the
train (III, 855), he did not consciously hear the train-
man's hammer tapping on the wheels. Yet later on it is
precisely that sound that provides the open-sesame for
total recall of the scene (III, 868). Why this apparent
absence of mind at presumably crucial moments?

In *Beyond the Pleasure Principle*, Freud speculates
that the elements of experience which enter consciousness do not leave memory traces. Consciousness provides
a "a protective shield" against stimuli—or at least a kind
of bypass for them. Only things we do not become con-
scious of make an imprint that may later be remembered. I find it a dismaying yet arresting theory. Is
Proust saying something similar? Does the obscure
mechanism, or muse, that activates our receptivity to
impressions and reminiscences operate only when left
free and unobserved? Does any effort on our part to
influence its working shut it off and float everything up
into the desiccating air of consciousness? In this view,
the only acceptable activity of mind for the artist is a
passive yielding to contingent forces around him. Many
critics have read the *Search* as the case history of a man
whose intense esthetic experiences issued from complete surrender to the present moment and from a systematic abasement of focused attention. But Proust goes
far beyond the absent-mindedness that Freud glimpsed
at the root of memory. He shows consciousness not as a
protective shield but as a mysterious vital process.[7]

---

[7] Another great restless mind had ventured this far into the
wilderness almost a century earlier. In the section of *Either/
Or* called "The Rotation Method," Kierkegaard anticipated
both Freud's doubts about the compatibility of memory and

To limit the scope of Proust's literary accomplishment to mental passivity would be like accepting "negative capability" as the full measure of Keats's genius. Neither writer can be so confined. The force and reach of their sensibilities do not shun polarities. I have already insisted on the factor of will power in Marcel's story. It

---

consciousness, and Proust's resolve to surmount any such frailty through a form of psychic delaying action, a stopping-to-look. Here is Kierkegaard:

> Enjoying an experience to its full intensity to the last minute will make it impossible either to remember or to forget. For there is then nothing to remember except a certain satiety, which one desires to forget, but which now comes back to plague the mind with an involuntary remembrance. Hence, when you begin to notice that a certain pleasure or experience is acquiring too strong a hold upon the mind, you stop for a moment for the purpose of remembering. No other method can better create a distaste for continuing the experience too long. From the beginning one should keep the enjoyment under control, never spreading every sail to the wind in any resolve; one ought to devote oneself to pleasure with a certain suspicion, a certain wariness, if one desires to give the lie to the proverb which says that no one can have his cake and eat it too. The carrying of concealed weapons is usually forbidden, but no weapon is so dangerous as the art of remembering. It gives one a very peculiar feeling in the midst of one's enjoyment to look back upon it for the purpose of remembering it. (*Either/Or*, trans. David F. Swenson and Lillian Marvin Swenson, Anchor Books, I, 289).

Watching from behind several ironic masks, Kierkegaard has seen everything. Yet he never claims final truth for any of his insights in this deeply cleft and antithetical work that refuses synthesis in any form. What he cannot do so well as Proust is to write a novel. "The Diary of a Seducer," the following section, runs aground on the lame category of "the interesting." Proust works in a different form and tone. Instead of holding them apart in separate volumes, he mixes his Either and his Or into a composite narrative line. Repeatedly along the way we are obliged to "stop a moment" in order, almost, to have our cake and eat it too.

Walter Benjamin touches on this general subject in his essay "On Some Motifs in Baudelaire."

reflects the choice that brought Proust to his full literary calling around 1909. At the beginning of the novel as at the end, the only real sickness afflicting Marcel attacks not his body but his will. The book hinges on the resolve Marcel discovers in himself. One has little difficulty in finding quotations that paint a very different portrait of the artist from the one in the preceding paragraphs. The number of texts Proust devoted to Baudelaire leaves little doubt about the tutelary role the poet played in the development of Proust's sensibility and his theories of memory. There is nothing unintentional about the closing words of Marcel's final meditation before entering the Guermantes's salon.

> In Baudelaire, finally, these reminiscences, more numerous even [than in Chateaubriand and Nerval], are less fortuituous and consequently, in my opinion, decisive. It is the poet himself who, with more choice than laziness,[8] deliberately sought, in a woman's odor, for example, in her hair or her breast, the inspiring analogies that will evoke in him "the azure of a vast encircling sky" and "a harbor thick with flames and masts" (III, 920).

Baudelaire's genius seems to have consisted in his capacity to apply choice and some kind of method to involuntary memory. In Marcel, Proust has created a figure in whose life the fortuitous and fleeting experiences of memory ultimately lead to a deliberately chosen self-dedication to literary art.

The passage quoted earlier on "the fortuitous and inevitable way" in which Marcel stumbled on the uneven paving stones (see above, page 120) is really incomplete. It belongs to a careful discussion of the sequence: impressions, reminiscences, art. The closing sentences cor-

[8] The printed text reads *"avec plus de choix et de paresse"*—an incoherent construction resolved by changing it to *"avec plus de choix que de paresse."* Gaëtan Picon certifies the correction, *Lecture de Proust,* p. 176.

rect many of the misconceptions I have been describing and speak not of passiveness but of *effort*.

> The impression is for the writer what experimentation is for the scientist, with this difference: that in the case of the scientist the work of the intelligence precedes, and in the case of the writer it comes after. Something we have not had to interpret, to illuminate by our personal effort, something that was clear before we arrived on the scene, is not truly ours. Only those things belong to us that we draw out of the obscurity inside us and that others do not know (III, 880).

In every instance of involuntary memory, from the Madeleine through the multiple series at the end, Marcel tries at least briefly to find an explanation of the phenomenon. Otherwise, it would not be *his* experience. Pulsing beneath the rich textures of the *Search* and expressive of Proust's whole attitude, I detect a movement toward the mastery of life which is stronger than his complementary moods of passive resignation to it.

The last quotation and a few earlier ones have already slipped into this discussion a set of terms which define a closely related and equally important opposition of forces. In many contexts Proust names and assigns contrasting functions to two mental faculties: *sensibility* (or imagination, feeling, instinct) and *intelligence*. It will not be sufficient to label the former passive and the latter active, though a loose parallel of this nature can be discerned. Because Marcel moved through a series of positions about the separation of powers between these putative faculties, and because Proust was too canny to have stayed very long with any schematic description of the human mind, one can demonstrate almost anything by quoting from the *Search*.[9]

[9] The same can be said of the implied opposition in the book between the concrete, highly individual, often monstrous events of the action, and the general laws which seem sometimes to describe and sometimes to govern them. On occasion

The tradition that divides thought into reason and faith, logic and feeling, goes back a very long way and may well coincide with that partial alienation from ourselves we call civilization. We should beware of these divisions and of the way they are reflected in our language and institutions. In using the terms of this dualism, Proust was not so much approving a conventional division of mind as attempting to reach the seat of thought by any means at hand. His writing—both his style and his story—implies that sensibility and intelligence are not distinct faculties but gradations along a continuous spectrum of mental process.

Now Proust never stops telling us that we can rarely possess or exercise all of our powers at once. According to the last quotation the scientist leads with his intellect, the writer or artist leads with his feeling or instinct. But Proust put forward other proposals. In the early treatment of these ideas that he rapped out as the preface to *Against Sainte-Beuve*, he appeals less to a chronological order of priority than to a subtle and nearly sophistical order of value.

> And as to this inferiority of the intelligence, one must still ask the intelligence to establish it. For if the intelligence does not deserve the supreme crown, it alone can bestow the crown. And if the intelligence holds only the second place in the hierarchy of virtues, it alone is capable of proclaiming that instinct must occupy the first place (*CSB*, 216).

The authority to bestow is also the authority to withhold. I know of few passages in Proust that appear so forthright and remain so ambivalent. This "hierarchy of virtues" is compromised by divided sovereignty. Proust's confidence rings hollow and conveys his frustration over the knottiness of the problem. He never really does solve

---

the Narrator sounds out of character. "Therefore it is useless to observe behavior, since one can deduce it from psychological laws" (I, 513).

it. Rather he dramatized the struggle in the *Search*. Marcel is profoundly torn until, at the end, the revelation of art lifts him bodily out of the impasse.

However, one passage deserves attention. It is frequently overlooked because it occurs in the midst of Marcel's troubled weighing of what course to follow when Albertine leaves him. Is she leaving him in order to stampede him into marriage? He considers this the first hypothesis, the intelligent one. Is she leaving him in order to take up again with her Lesbian playmates? This is the second hypothesis, the instinctive one. He is drawn powerfully to the second.

> But—and what follows will make it even clearer, as many episodes have already suggested it—the fact that the intelligence is not the subtlest, the most powerful and appropriate instrument for grasping the truth, is only one more reason for beginning with the intelligence, and not with an unconscious intuition, not with an unquestioned faith in presentiments. It is life itself which, little by little, case by case, allows us to notice that what is most important for our heart, for our mind [*esprit*], is taught us not by reasoning but by other powers. And then it is the intelligence itself which, acknowledging their superiority, abdicates, by reasoning, before them, and accepts the role of becoming their collaborator and servant. Experimental faith (III, 423).

It is a stunning text, studded with crucial words: *vie*, *esprit*, *foi*, *expérimentale*. The order of events is totally reversed here. Our intelligence must set our existential priorities not after but *before* the fact. On faith. *Reasoned faith*. We come inevitably to paradox, close to the paradoxes of theology. As it is reasonable to have faith in the impressions of childhood, it is reasonable to have faith in presentiments and other feelings that seek the truth. But that faith is experimental. It lies open to the examination and judgment of intelligence. We come back then to an alternation of states or stages, with the implication that reason has both the first and the last say. From his quest for the seat of thought Proust returned with this short version of a long journey: *foi expérimentale*. Scientific belief. Faith-filled experiment. Intelligence and intuition working together, checking and encouraging one another. The *Search* shows a man trying to find his mind —his whole mind. Often it seems to have two opposed parts. Like Plato's charioteer, he learns to control his two steeds and make them pull as one.

COMPOSITION

Against his better judgment Proust accepted serial publication of his novel. Only a little more than half the volumes were published in his lifetime. When the first installment appeared in 1913 with its misleading, false-bottom ending (see below, page 152n), Proust was fully aware that one part would not go very far toward conveying a sense of the whole. At the end of the *Search* he has the Narrator complain bitterly about the reception of *his* early sketches: "No one understood a thing" (III, 1041). In spite of a few discerning critics and his own patient explanations, the complaint applied generally in Proust's case.

His first professional reader (for the Fasquelle publishing house) called the first volume "wandering" and asked irritably in his report: "What's it all about?" He concluded that the book was written by a "pathological case." One of the most perceptive of Proust's recent critics, Deleuze, doesn't sound very different when he insists that the novel's subject is Time: ". . . it brings with it fragments which can no longer be restored, pieces which do not fit into the same puzzle, which do not belong to a preceding totality, which do not emanate from the same lost unity." Proust, on the other hand, never tired of insisting on the unity and totality of his novel. To Louis de Robert he asserted that it displays "very strict composition, though not easy to grasp because of its complexity." As sovereign proof, he frequently cited the fact that the first page and the last page were written together, a demonstration of the convergence or circular form of the story. Is there any way in which these conflicting opinions can be reconciled? One device Proust adopted in the *Search*, to express conflicting principles of fragmentation and unity, is the double *I*. Inside it, Marcel's projects keep going astray and dispersing under the ordering, reflective gaze of the Narrator. The double *I* creates a narrative iridescence that does not resolve itself until the end. But we shall have to explore the questions of unity and composition more carefully.

The opening fifty-page section of the *Search* moves through three distinct stages. The first three pages record the thoughts of an unidentified and unlocated consciousness trying to orient itself while wandering on the frontier between waking and sleep. As it seeks its identity, it describes a movement backward and downward in the evolution of consciousness through sickness, childhood, Edenic innocence, the ignorance of a cave man, and animal existence, to nothingness—*le néant*. When rescued by memory from this collapse, the narrative voice says: "In a second I passed through centuries of civilization" (I, 5). In the most literal and direct sense, the *Search* opens, like *Alice in Wonderland*, with a fall. Consciousness tumbles all the way back to a point before cave men, before creation itself, to the void. The book recoils to zero. Then out of the swirl of images one scene comes clear. It is the second stage. A child in Combray is anxiously awaiting his mother's goodnight kiss. But that vivid spot of awareness cannot expand beyond a strict limit. It remains blocked until the spell is broken in the third stage. Through the unexpected intervention of the *madeleine* incident, a whole segment of the past comes back and gives the protagonist a firm identity, the start of a life, and a story to follow.

Correspondingly at the end of the novel, the narrative comes to a conclusion in three stages. After his long

wanderings Marcel arrives at the last Guermantes reception and experiences a series of reminiscences explicitly
echoing the *madeleine* sequence (III, 866). They too
seem to array the past around him, this time as available
material for his literary undertakings. The second stage
carries him into the salon. Suddenly, all his projects fall
apart because he cannot recognize anyone. For an
agonizing interval he is locked back into the present, into
contingency. It takes a hundred pages for Marcel to
readjust his sights and to focus on past and present
together. Then he moves to the third stage not through
any phenomenon of memory but by recognizing his role
and resolving to write his book. Whereas the imagery
of the opening implied a fall and partial recovery, the
end raises an old man on the stilts of age and time,
awaiting death.[10]

What can we now make of Proust's insistence that the
last page of the novel "comes back exactly to the first"?
A little reflection shows that the three stages of the
opening and those of the close occur in reverse order. In
the first chapter: wandering consciousness seeking identity; the clear outlines of a specific scene; and the release
of involuntary memory. In the last chapter: the release
of involuntary memory; the clear outlines of a specific
scene; and a detached consciousness settling down to
write. In both sequences the second stage works as an
obstacle. Marcel is held captive in a single segment of
contingent time until a new development releases him.
But the narrative movement in these two segments is
flowing in opposite directions. Is there some kind of
pattern here?

In a letter to Mme Scheikévitch in 1915 Proust tran-
scribed nearly verbatim from his novel in progress a

[10] My analysis here owes a good deal to the chapter on Proust
in Jean Rousset's *Form et Signification*. However, where he
sees two stages I see three. And we have markedly different
ideas about the relation between the opening and the close
of the novel.

description of the way Marcel fell in and out of love with Albertine (III, 558). "Before forgetting her completely, like a traveler who comes back to his point of departure by the same route, . . . I had to pass through all the same feelings I had already gone through—but in reverse order." The shape of the action now comes into view. The beginning and the end of the novel are firmly in place, the former leading us into and the latter out of the narrative. In between comes a malleable and infinitely expandable section, which did in fact more than triple its original size. This vast median segment has the resilience of life itself. No incident seems absolutely essential; all are significant when related to the rest. The opening and the close establish beyond challenge an overarching movement that encompasses all digressions and meanderings. After the initial and transient hope of salvation in childhood, the *Search* follows a downward slope toward error, perdition, and death. Only at the end does the action turn out to be a resurrection. And now we may be able to discern why Proust insisted not on the distance but on the closeness between the first page and the last.

A number of modern novels concern a character who is at work writing a novel. A literary convention has grown up implying that we are reading that fictional novel. The convention has something both obvious and contrived about it. A few years after Proust's death, Gide's *The Counterfeiters* and Huxley's derivative *Point Counter Point* developed the scheme into a sustained spoof of the novel form. They seem to say ad infinitum, This is a novel about writing a novel about. . . . Sensing the fragility as well as the fascination of that theme, Proust held it off until the very end of his work. Marcel, we are repeatedly told, will never be a writer. Yet when at the end, against all odds and expectations, he metamorphoses into the Narrator of his own life, a whole new state of things appears. The shift takes place, of course, only if we have read the novel for ourselves and do not come armed with the interpretations of ambitious critics (inescapably, I am one) anxious to tell us what it all means. Proust's ending leads us firmly out of the *Search* as Marcel's story and across into a symmetrical mirror-novel, consisting of all the same words and incidents, giving the Narrator's story. A new circumambulation begins, this time not of living the events but of writing them.

Proust's construction of his novel could now be traced out in graphic form. The firmly established paths marking the opening and close permit almost limitless latitude in the intermediate sections. And the careful alignment of the entry with the exit, retracing the same steps in reverse order, leads us over into a second reading or interpretation of the same text as an act of narrative composition after it has first been the story of a man's life (see Diagram V).

Through the literary account B, which has the advan-

V. SHAPE AND TRAJECTORY OF THE *SEARCH*

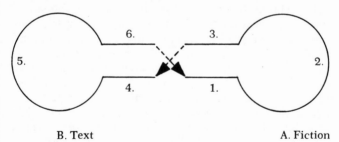

B. Text   A. Fiction

	Life	{	1.	Three stages of *Combray* (first fifty pages)
A.	*as*	{	2.	Vagaries of Marcel's life
	failure	{	3.	Three stages at the close of *Time Regained* (two hundred pages)

	Narrative	4. }		The same incidents as 1, 2, and 3
B.	*as*	5. }		seen not as Marcel's present
	success	6. }		but as the Narrator's past.

tage over life of being transparent and temporally plastic, we look at the fictive life A, Marcel's remembered experiences as he grows up. Occasionally as we read we become aware of B, the account itself, with its cross references, stage whispers, signal flags, and demurrers. Insofar as we do pay attention to B revealing A, we accept a relation between the two as one of translation. Ideally, during an innocent first reading, the effect of the double *I* keeps one's attention generally fixed on A, Marcel's story. We watch love and friendship, social success and even art disintegrate as he reaches them. Only at the very end does the reader follow Marcel in performing a great double take on what has happened. No major new element enters the action. Chance alone intervenes in the humble form of paving stones and spoons and water pipes. Yet everything Marcel has gone through has slowly and imperceptibly shifted the odds in his favor until chance has the force of fate. He lives surrounded by signs and secrets. Suddenly, *qui perd gagne*: loser takes all. By an act of recognition which incorporates rather than rejects lived experience, Marcel sees the past anew as his own, as himself. It is the moment at which he becomes the Narrator, thus finding the vocation which he presumed totally lost.

This metamorphosis in Marcel brings about the transition from A to B in the form of a setting to work. Retroactively it transforms every event of A into a new pattern *of success*, the systematic changing of signs permitted by the vantage point of age and retelling. This new light shed back over the entire action implies a second reading, this time not of A but of B. For as originally B reveals A, now A reveals B. Ideally again, two readings are implied. Yet a skilled reader will read A and B simultaneously, even if he can take advantage only of the clues given him in the text. For example, how can Marcel's sensibility and his alertness to his own flickering states of mind (doubted and belittled in A; recorded in B) simply wither away as A keeps saying? The richness of the prose one is reading, as well as the long detour through painting and music which sustains Marcel's interest in art, imply the contrary.

It is precisely this firm construction that is lacking in Proust's earlier attempts at large-scale fiction. Having only a highly contrived beginning and no end, *Jean Santeuil* gives the effect of being all middle. The motley of texts lumped together under the awkward title, *Against Saint-Beuve* reveals Proust's impatience to find a form that would contain both events and reflections on events. The preface he drafted for that project shows how far astray Proust still was in early 1909, even though he had collected most of his essential ideas and incidents, including the resurrections. He opens the preface with three rapid pages narrating the three classic resurrections: toast dipped in tea, uneven paving stones, the clink of spoon on a plate. The incidents barely receive their due, and the exposition quickly moves on to other matters. It appears that Proust did not know what use to make of these importunings of involuntary memory and simply blurted them all out at the beginning. Within a few months, however, he had changed his scheme completely and saved the resurrections for the *end* of a story which he would eventually name *In Search of Lost Time*. In order to give the reader one clue to go on, one anticipation of the end, Proust left the tea and toast (or *madeleine*) sequence in place, near the opening. The others are transferred to the new location. Now we can see that the first pages of preface to *Against Sainte-Beuve* contain in germ both the opening and the close of the *Search*, but with no sense of a life lived in between. They read like a manifesto on memory, creating no undertow of narrative.

For the *Search*, Proust found the arrangement that allowed him to tell a story. The theme of great expectations runs very strong at the start and then diminishes, leaving us adrift on the ocean of Marcel's desultory life. The ocean seems to go on forever, until, when we have given up hope of any further movement, we find that the current is running again and has carried us back to shore—the same shore we left, now transformed by the passage of time.

This narrative line makes strict demands on the timing by which things can be divulged. The truth must not come out too soon. The limitation goes far beyond that of Marcel's age and experience. The end of the story controls all other sections. For example, in the first volume one of the guests at the Verdurins' dinners is a vulgar, ambitious, seemingly untalented painter called Monsieur Tiche or Biche. In later volumes the dedicated artist Elstir initiates Marcel to the genuine rewards of painting. Toward the end of *Within a Budding Grove*, Marcel discovers that Tiche and Elstir are the same man. While revising *Sodom and Gomorrah*, Proust decided that this discovery comes much too soon and made an urgent note for himself.

> *Nota Bene.* Don't say in this volume that Mme Verdurin called him Monsieur Tiche, nor, secondly, that I [i.e., Marcel] understand it's the same man whose life I learned about earlier. Keep the first for the Goncourt passage, and the second for the last chapter (II, 1200).

He never had time to make the necessary changes, but the sense of narrative shape he was aiming at is clear.

At the same time Proust could not abandon his readers entirely to Marcel's shrinking world of false scents and disappointments. At intervals along the spiral stairway of the narrative, we come upon a narrow window from which we can see a fleck of the countryside that later we will see in its full expanse from the top. These anticipatory glimpses do not fit together into a single picture, but they encourage our climbing. The first such window occurs early when Marcel flees from the scene in which his great-aunt exasperated his grandmother by urging his grandfather to drink more than he should.

Alas! I didn't know that, much more grievously than
these little weaknesses of her husband, my lack of will
power, my delicate health, and the uncertainty they
shed over my future, preoccupied my grandmother as
she incessantly paced about morning and evening
(I, 12).

Narrative has its own form of preterition. Proust's "I
didn't know" is a fairly crude way of smuggling a fragment of contraband information into the text. He can
do better. The concert of Elstir's septet, occurring two
thirds of the way through the novel, is a subtle and ambitious extension of the same hortatory device. When
both the reader and Marcel need it badly, the scene
anticipates esthetic rewards still to come.

Aside from these brief remissions to keep us moving
along, the *Search* flows powerfully within the confines
of its double loop. Marcel and the Narrator attain their
respective goals, the one of finding and assuming his
full identity, the other of writing an account of that
achievement. As Diagram V seems to say in its very
appearance, this circular construction does not appeal
beyond life fully lived to any higher domain—a world of
eternal verities, a divine being, or the historic destiny of
man. Proust's story of self-rehabilitation makes a very
human and earth-bound document. It does not hesitate
to invoke any resource men have tried in order to sustain
their faith, including the transmigration of souls and the
legend of *le peuple éternel*. However, they are transient
appeals. The reflexive architecture of the novel informs
us that memory and art will lead us not out of life but
back to it.

MEMORY

To endure, to keep the faith entails some form of continuity with the past. Men have ritual, ideology, and
institutions to serve the purpose. When Scott Moncrieff
translated *A la recherche du temps perdu* as *Remem-*

brance of Things Past (after Shakespeare's Sonnet 30),
he was being clumsily explicit about expressing the special form of continuity explored in this case history:
memory. So many different affective processes hide
behind that simple word that I must begin by distinguishing them.

The *Search* follows a rough chronological order of
stages in Marcel's life that corresponds to an emerging
intellectual order of significance and reward. At the start
the most vivid segment of Marcel's world is made up of
impressions. They are isolated perceptions of the natural
world, which discover an indefinable yet almost palpable
aura of significance in the ordinary objects and places
that provoke them. Such moments bring Marcel a feeling of happiness and a heightened sense of reality; they
seem to ask for some kind of response. Yet the response
usually aborts, and the moment passes. It is worth looking at a specific instance of these impressions.

Marcel, not yet in his teens, is taking one of his cus-
tomary autumn walks "out Swann's way" after a morning's reading. Both the landscape and the windy weather
seem to answer his need for animated motion after a
sedentary morning. Every feeling in him seeks immediate release. The whole tradition of the promenade, from
Petrarch to Rousseau to Rimbaud, hovers over this carefully constructed page. Proust frames the sensuous description of the scene between accounts of two human
discrepancies: the inadequacy of our actions and words
to express our feelings, and the contrast between the
feelings of different people reacting to the same situation. Those discrepancies cause deep frustration in Marcel at the time. For he perceives a delicate pattern of
elements that gives the scene, for his sensibility and
possibly for no one else's, a wondrous beauty. In the first
two sentences, the Narrator is speaking; then he dis-
solves into Marcel in a perfect case of the double *I*. I
quote the scene in full:

When we attempt to translate our feelings into expression, we usually do no more than relieve ourselves
of them by letting them escape in an indistinct form
which tells us nothing about them. When I try to
reckon up all that I owe to the "Méséglise way," all the
humble discoveries of which it was either the acci-
dental setting or the direct inspiration and cause, I
am reminded that it was that same autumn, on one
of those walks near the bushy slope that overlooks
Montjouvain, that I was struck for the first time by
this lack of harmony between our impressions and
their normal forms of expression. After an hour of
rain and wind, against which I had put up a brisk
fight, as I came to the edge of the Montjouvain pond
and reached a little hut, roofed with tiles, in which
M. Vinteuil's gardener kept his tools, the sun shone
out again, and its golden rays, washed clean by the
shower, gleamed once more in the sky, on the trees,
on the wall of the hut, and on the still wet tiles of
the roof, where a chicken was walking along the ridge.
The wind pulled out sideways the wild grass that grew
in the wall as well as the chicken's downy feathers,
both of which floated out to their full length in the
wind's breath with the unresisting submissiveness of
flimsy lifeless things. The tiled roof showed in the
pond, whose reflections were now clear again in the
sunlight, as a pink marbled area such as I had
never noticed before. And, when I saw both on the
water and on the surface of the wall a pale smile
answering the smile in the sky, I cried aloud in my
enthusiasm and excitement while brandishing my
furled umbrella, "Gosh, gosh, gosh, gosh."

And it was at that moment too—thanks to a peasant
who went by, apparently in a bad enough humor
already, but who became even more so when he nearly
got a poke in the face from my umbrella, and who
barely replied to my "What a fine day! Good to be out
walking!"—that I learned that identical emotions do
not arise in the hearts of all men simultaneously
according to a pre-established order (I, 155).

Movement, light, and texture compose a landscape as unified as a Corot painting. Marcel recognizes it as such. The Narrator describes it in an accelerating paragraph that seeks to follow the rapid motion of Marcel's glance. The dynamics of light and wind are forceful enough to connect all elements of roof, pond, and sky within Marcel's sensibility as a set of Baudelairean correspondences. For a moment the "border" of consciousness is lifted. Then come the umbrella flourishing and the childish exclamations to passing peasants. Inevitably, the Narrator brings out the comic side of Marcel's frustration before so great beauty. After this, the Narrator drops the scene as if it were an unattached detail, a fortuitous moment of delight, transitory because it fits into no established sequence and leads nowhere. A few pages later, he explains.

> It was certainly not impressions of this kind that could restore the hope I had lost of succeeding one day in becoming an author and a poet, for each of them was associated with some material object devoid of any intellectual value, and suggesting no abstract truth (I, 179).

Though they continue to provoke a deep personal response in him, Marcel turns his back on his impressions. Only later does he realize that they are the very stuff of reality and have prepared him for the two later stages of memory: *resurrection-reminiscence* (Proust uses the Christian and the Greek terms interchangeably; I shall do likewise), and *art*.

An impression re-encountered after a sufficient interval for forgetting may provoke a resurrection, a close relative of *déjà vu*. A resurrection may or may not lead to recognition of the original impression or memory trace. When it does, a revelation ensues which is even more gratifying then the simple impression. In the *madeleine* passage near the opening of the *Search*, Proust depicts reminiscence as an overpowering recollection of the Narrator's past in all its "form and solidity" (I, 48). At the end of the novel, resurrections are assigned the even greater power of affording us a glimpse of "the essences of things." Without being explicit, Proust implies that the mental functions that permit reminiscences to occur exist at least potentially in all men, and that we have probably experienced them without paying much attention. They are a form of true spiritual experience, without reliance on a divine being or on the miraculous. They signify the existence of a realm of awareness beyond the ordinary. Marcel's resurrections are usually accompanied by his exhortations to himself to "go beyond the moment," to "get to the bottom of" (*"approfondir"*) the experience. From his friends' accounts we know that Proust's own reminiscences were so acute as to constitute a form of hyperesthesia. By attributing this condition to Marcel, he made it crucial to the novel.

The most condensed explanation of involuntary memory can be found in a scene where the process fails to occur. Late in life Marcel revisits Combray.

> I found the Vivonne narrow and ugly along the towpath. Not that I noticed particularly great inaccuracies in what I remembered. But, separated by a whole lifetime from places I now happened to pass through again, there did not exist between them and me that contiguity out of which is born, before one even notices it, the immediate, delicious, and total flaming up [*déflagration*] of memory (III, 692).[11]

Though he switches terms disconcertingly, Proust here does not depart from the principles by which Hume, and

[11] As we know from several other passages on successful resurrections, what Proust refers to in the above passage as "contiguity" really means *similarity* between a material object in the present and one in a past impression. The real Vivonne does not resemble his childhood impression of it. He probably says contiguity here because similarity is felt subjectively as a closeness, a near relation.

after him Bergson, deal with the association of states of consciousness. Hume recognized the relations of *contiguity* (in the temporal aspects of simultaneity or close succession and the spatial aspect of proximity) and *similarity*, and devoted much of his career to an attempt to reduce a third principle, causation, to a special case of succession. In his second book, *Matter and Memory* (1896), Bergson picks up Hume's terms. He even puts forward a capsule version of Gestalt theory by insisting that our first perceptions come in "an aggregate of contiguous parts" and that the primary mental process is one of dissociation from "the undivided unity of perception." Usually our psychological life oscillates between similarity and contiguity. Yet in one key passage Bergson suggests that the two processes may work together. ". . . once the memory trace has been connected [by similarity] to the present perception, a multitude of events contiguous to the memory trace immediately attach themselves to the perception."

In passages of phenomenological description whose ideas and introspective tone anticipate Proust's writing, Bergson argues that pure or spontaneous memory is "independent of our will." Both men describe how a tiny link of similarity between present and past can provoke a sudden spreading of recollection to all contiguous elements—Proust's "deflagration." The power of involuntary memory lies in combining two associative principles.[12] Similarity triggers contiguity, and the explosion blasts a whole segment of contiguous past events into the present. The force of this explosion stops Marcel in

[12] Gérard Genette has written a penetrating article on this subject: "Métonymie chez Proust," *Poétique*, no. 2, 1970. He borrows his terms from the linguist Roman Jakobson who, in an article on aphasia, equates metaphor with similarity and metonomy with contiguity. By using the rhetorical terms Genette makes a good case for the hybrid state of Proust's work as both realism and poetry. In order to comprehend the phenomenon of reminiscence in Proust, I find it wise to stay with the philosophical terms.

his tracks and elevates him to a state approaching felicity. He comes back to contingent reality only with great difficulty and reluctance.

The impressions and the reminiscences which resurrect them resemble polished gems which the rest of Proust's prose seems to set off with its lower relief. Both the psychological intensity they produce and the poetic style in which they are written attest to their special status. The drafts of the novel reveal that Proust conceived most of these passages very early, revised and perfected them through many versions, and finally did set them like precious stones in the surface of the narrative. As he states explicitly many times, he found precedent and confirmation for his experiences of memory in a number of his favorite authors: Nerval, Chateaubriand, Baudelaire, George Eliot, Ruskin. Each of them depicts a particular mode and mood by which the present comes into phase with the past. But in order to examine the nature of memory in Proust, I shall refer to two philosophers, one ancient and one modern.[13]

---

[13] Two sidelights on the subject of Proust and memory deserve brief mention.

The eminent Russian neurologist and psychologist A. R. Luria has written an absorbing study of the vaudeville mnemonist, S., who could memorize almost anything and never forget it. Certain aspects of his case seem to relate to Proust's, or at least to the experience of memory Proust projects in the *Search*. S.'s memory was basically nonverbal and highly synesthetic. Out of professional necessity, S. had developed a technique for remembering items, including words, by distributing them along a kind of mental walk or improvised story. Thus linked, these images "reconstructed themselves whenever he revived the original situation in which something had been registered in his memory." *The Mind of a Mnemonist.* Lynn Solotaroff, trans. (New York, 1968), p. 63. It might almost be a systematized reminiscence. The differences may be even more revealing. S. developed his memory by long training and careful attention to items given to him to remember. Proust insisted on the primacy of involuntary memory and implied that attention upsets the mechanism. Nevertheless, in the course of the novel Marcel develops

Beginning in the *Meno* Plato developed a theory of knowledge based on reminiscence. Its greatest importance was to deny the empirical origin of knowledge from sense experience. True knowledge is understood to mean true beliefs dialectically rooted in the logical reasons for their truth. And those reasons, as the *Meno* demonstrates, are found within us by *remembering*. We may remember from an earlier existence; Plato's first affirmation of the doctrine of the transmigration of souls comes in this dialogue. The theory of Ideas, developed later, is his response to the question of how the soul attains knowledge in the first place. The significant element here is that Plato discredits empirical knowledge or sense observation in favor of the recognition or recollection of logical relationships.[14] Truly to know something means reconciling past and present experience; the soul's bumpy journey through previous lives greatly extends the reservoir of past experience available to our present lives. Proust had studied Plato and was familiar with this nexus of ideas.

I have already mentioned Bergson. *Matter and Memory* appeared with great éclat when Proust was twenty-five. Its blend of phenomenological description, scientific attitude, philosophical intent, and lucid style must have been irresistible to a young author who was already

---

a kind of negative technique in which successful *forgetting* serves as the prelude to later retrieval. Marcel has to forget and later remember his grandmother's death in order to feel its reality. He even has to forget his vocation in order to find it. Proust was a mnemonist looking the other way.

In *Proust's Binoculars* (New York, 1963), pp. 148–49, I discuss Dr. Wilder Penfield's experiments in surgical stimulation of the brain under local anesthetic. His patients experienced flashes of total recall whose "reality" rivaled or surpassed that of actuality. These experiments are the nearest neurological confirmation we have of Proust's theories of memory. (See also Justin O'Brien's article in *PMLA*, March 1970.)

[14] Gregory Vlastos, "Anamnesis in the Meno," has helped me understand Plato's argument, *Dialogue*, IV, 2, 1965.

absorbed in closely related problems of subjective experience. In his second chapter, Bergson spends fifteen pages distinguishing two forms of memory. "The memory of habit" enables us to develop a series of motor responses to present reality and to learn how to cope with our environment. "Pure or spontaneous memory" occurs when a chance event disturbs the equilibrium established by habit and brings back the complete image of a past moment still stamped with "a date and a place." In the third chapter, Bergson examines the various ways in which these two forms of memory interpenetrate and tend to fuse in ordinary experience. Despite Proust's widely accepted statements to the contrary (see Appendix, page 170), the distinction between voluntary and involuntary memories is basic to Bergson's argument. For example:

> This spontaneous memory, which no doubt lurks behind acquired or habitual memory, can reveal itself in sudden flashes: but it withdraws at the tiniest movement of voluntary memory.

Bergson's steady and highly sensitive scrutiny of memory is masterful, an essential complement to the commonly cited "classic" on the subject, F. C. Bartlett's experimentally based *Remembering*.[15]

Furthermore, Bergson makes memory the central principle of his psychology, very nearly the equivalent of Freud's unconscious. Everything seems to depend on the way we deploy the two kinds of memory. The basic processes of adaptation grow out of it, as well as our mental health, our character, and our oscillation between contrasting mental states. Bergson constantly uses ideas and turns of phrase that belong to the spiritual world of Proust, even the term "resurrection." What strikes one particularly in *Matter and Memory* is Bergson's strong interest in pure or spontaneous memory.

[15] *Remembering: A Study in Experimental and Social Psychology* (New York, 1932).

Toward the end, he argues that withdrawing attention from life and abandoning oneself to spontaneous memory amounts to the state of dreaming, and "dream in every respect imitates insanity." Bergson keeps a firm hold on the *juste milieu*. But earlier passages do not hide a deep fascination with "the storehouse of memories" and the circumstances that bring them into play.[16] Proust's denials of Bergson's influence can only be termed disingenuous.

Plato, Bergson, and Proust assemble in the vicinity of the philosophical conviction that a single direct sense perception does not suffice to furnish right knowledge. Though they describe contrasting ways in which sense perceptions combine into pairs and patterns, none of them describes association taking place without the individual's interests and volition playing a crucial role. Recognition, recollection, binocular vision, stereo-reception in time—all these modes characterize our mental processes. A wholly unique sensation remains alien until assimilated by one or more of them. Consciousness in full command of its powers is double or even multiple— divided between waking and sleep (as in the opening of the *Search*), between habit and disruption by the unfamiliar (as in many of the middle sections), between past and present (toward the end). The crucial moments in the *Search* belong to composite states. Proust presents the resurrections of involuntary memory as the most complex and the most rewarding.

Proust's epistemology could be called Platonic insofar as he echoes the doctrine of reminiscence as the source

---

[16] Bergson occasionally even sounds like Proust. This sentence recalls one of Proust's near the opening of the novel and glows with the same sympathy for certain privileged subjective states. Bergson: "A human being who *dreamed* his life instead of living it would probably thus keep constantly in sight the infinite multitude of details of his past history." Proust: "A sleeping man keeps arrayed in a circle around him the stream of hours, the ordering of years and worlds" (I, 5).

of true knowledge, and Bergsonian insofar as he distinguishes two kinds of memory—spontaneous-involuntary and habitual-voluntary. The parts of Plato's and Bergson's thinking that he dismissed are equally significant. Though deeply tempted by reincarnation as an ancient myth and metaphor for human transcendence (e.g., I, 3 and II, 985), Proust appealed to it only in highly poetic terms and generally confined memory to the dimensions of a single human life. Though he makes frequent use of the term "essence" in conjunction with intelligence, he never posits a supreme set of entities comparable to Plato's Ideas. Proust is usually careful to cast his allusions to transcendent entities and experiences in metaphorical style. Yet he refuses to accept the strict continuity of *la durée*, the temporal mode of Bergson's intuition. In the *Search* the twinge of involuntary memory is portrayed as surmounting contingency by an act that is not continuous with *la durée* but that overleaps it. The book as a whole has a fall/redemption pattern that seems to beg for spiritual interpretation. Though Proust proposes no deity, and no direct experience that transcends human life, many critics have come to the conclusion that the basic orientation of his work is religious and that mystical experience, as described in the resurrections, provides the impetus for his novel.

R. C. Zaehner devotes a cool-headed chapter to Proust in his book, *Mysticism, Sacred and Profane*. Zaehner believes that Proust had had "the natural mystical experience." Proust does not attribute it to an apprehension of God and carefully analyzes its occurrences along lines which, according to Zaehner, approach descriptions of Zen *satori*. My own view parallels Zaehner's. I believe Proust was in search of an integration of his sense of self beyond the pure present. In spite of some slippage in vocabulary and in figures of speech, his most elevated passages are not properly speaking religious but physiological and psychological, based on the secular experience of impressions and resurrections. They concern his earthly life. Death is final; metempsychosis, however alluring and even "reasonable," remains a "Celtic belief" (I, 44). Impressions and resurrections can be considered "spiritual" in several senses of the word. Proust values them highly enough to have made them a major theme in a long novel that can indeed be read as a spiritual exercise. But the novel's fall-redemption theme grows out of the basic movement of forgetting-remembering. It should not be given religious or transcendent meaning beyond that of developing a heightened mental capacity to respond to such experiences.

From a very early age, then, Proust lived with impressions and reminiscences. These moments overflowed with psychic and spiritual significance, yet there was something missing. For years Proust could not discover a direct and essential relation between their potency and the other major country of the mind that absorbed him: art and literature.

Several passages in *Jean Santeuil* relate a struggle to grasp the origin and significance of moments of total recall or *déjà vu*. In the most striking of them, Jean wonders why the sight of Lake Geneva from his carriage one afternoon not only reminds him of the ocean in Brittany but also "raises him up out of the slavery of the present and floods [him] with the sentiment of a permanent life" (*JS*, 402). But his reflections about essence and imagination seem to be stillborn.

The notebooks of about 1908 suggest that Proust had not advanced much further. He was still swinging indecisively between a hollow social life and desultory writing. Even a newly found gift for literary pastiche did not relieve his general discouragement.

As soon as I read an author, I perceived the melodic line which is different in every artist. . . . But I have not used that gift, and from time to time at different periods of my life, I have felt it still alive in me, like that other gift of discovering a deep-seated connection between two ideas, two sensations. It is still alive but not strengthened, and it will soon weaken and die (*CSB*, 303).

In this instance Proust specifically associated his literary capacities with his moments of intense mnemonic association—but only to call them both failures.

The *Search* follows a parallel trajectory. The impressions and, even more intensely, the rare resurrections release great psychic force into Marcel's consciousness. But they lead nowhere and they remain transitory. They allow a glimpse of a higher, more permanent reality, but no permanent abode. In *The Captive*, Marcel finally loses confidence in the one talisman he has been carrying for many years, the experience of the *madeleine*. "Nothing assured me that the vagueness of such states was a sign of their profundity" (III, 382). His strongest insights lock him into a deeper solitude than ever. He can share these moments with no one. His inner life isolates him even more than the false scents of love and social climbing. "The universe is real for all of us, and different for each one of us" (III, 191). It is a desperately forlorn sentence. Marcel's difference, i.e., his mnemonic gift, brings him isolation as its only reward.

ART

Somewhere along the way, when he should have been coming into his own, Proust fell very low. His gifts seemed to fail him. In the novel Marcel reaches an equally dismal point. Both survived and achieved salvation through art. It had been there all along. We shall have to search through both stories again in order to discover how it happened.

In the opening chapter, I touched on the perplexities and moral insecurity of Proust's existence as he entered his late thirties. He had no job, no wife, no firm social status, no sure sense of past or future accomplishments. He had published one book of youthful fragments, about which he had ambivalent feelings, two translations of an author whose intellectual posture he had rejected, and a few semijournalistic texts. But the bulk of his writing lay buried in a stack of notebooks. By his own exacting standards he was a failure; by outward appearances he was a wealthy amateur and a social sycophant. Nevertheless, he kept trying. In the latter part of 1908, Proust announced to his friends that he was working on a new project: an essay, combined somehow with a personal narrative, on Sainte-Beuve's critical method. In the second sentence of the preface he drafted for the work, he states flatly that "past impressions" form "the only materials of Art" (*CSB*, 211). But after a brief discussion of the "resurrection" of three such impressions, he moves on into an ambivalent and unfinished discourse on the role of the intelligence in literature. *Against Sainte-Beuve*, as this project came to be called, assembles the old materials once again and tries to arrange them in a kind of circle around a half-dreaming consciousness in a bedroom. Proust put the project aside within a year—or rather he incorporated it into something significantly different. For, during the first half of 1909, Proust resolved his personal and artistic crisis and redeemed much of the writing he thought he had been producing to no purpose.

At this point Proust was traveling on two kinds of moral credit: his declining theories about the experience of involuntary memory (by now confirmed in his reading of Bergson's first two books); and the growing conviction that suffering and grief are ultimately salutary and provide a form of spiritual knowledge. Both sets of ideas turned Proust back toward his own past and encouraged him to see it with augmented relief, with depth perception in time. Both involuntary memory and the "agitations of grief" raise up out of the mind a landscape of thoughts and feelings that otherwise lies at too low a level to be seen (III, 897). In one direction these clues led backward in time toward one crucial incident that

held the germ of everything to some. They took Proust
to *le drame du coucher* (the goodnight scene), a play
within a play enacting the ritual of desire and discon-
tent that animates soul error. But the same forces of
memory and grief also led Proust in the opposite direction, forward toward the present in its relation to the
future.

What happened represented a distinct mental leap.
Sometime in 1909 Proust grasped that his story was the
very process of failure and rediscovery that he was going
through. His book lay at his feet. He must watch and
tread carefully. For his present turmoil over memory
and art projected his theme, both the message and
method of a novel. He reached beyond autobiography
toward the transformation of his life into the shape of
a story that could convey his deepest sense of self. He
discovered the device, or the design, of what could be
called *a play outside a play.* By seeing his personal
situation from outside as if it radiated a larger, generalized narrative action of loss and recovery, he transformed his failure into potential success and his isolation
into communication. Thus he discovered the unity of
form fatally absent in *Jean Santeuil* and *Against Sainte-
Beuve.* What the draft preface of the latter of those texts
states vainly at the start, the *Search* affirms triumph-
antly at its close. "I understood that those materials for
a literary work were my own past life" (III, 899). This
insight of 1909 signifies a shift away from both autobiography and fiction (as pure invention) to *translation*,
a term that keeps occurring in the final section of the
Search. Henceforward, Proust became the author of his
own life and also of a book which subsumed his life.
Increasingly he gave priority to the latter, to his work,
for which the former became a rehearsal subject to
observation and experiment. Proust produced a work of
art representing as its subject the circumstances and
vagaries of its own creation and the origin of its form.
Proust detected something comparable to this *play*

outside a play effect in the work of three nineteenth-century authors. The separate books of Balzac, Hugo, and Michelet, he observes, fail to sustain the powerful schemes those authors invented later (and expressed in prefaces) to create one massive work encompassing the individual volumes.

> . . . watching themselves work as if they were both workman and judge, [these authors] drew out of that self-contemplation a new form of beauty exterior and superior to the work, imposing a retroactive unity on it, a grandeur it does not have (III, 160).

With some qualifications I accept Proust's implication that his work does have the unity and grandeur which Balzac, Hugo, and Michelet failed to achieve. Proust's expanded vision of his life as the source of his work came in time to allow him to recast his earlier work and project the vision over writings to come. His equivalent of a preface describing his "subsequent unity" (III, 161) is contained inside the novel in passages like the one just quoted.

This reorientation in Proust's writing resembles an inversion of the figure-ground relation in painting. In *Jean Santeuil* neutral stretches of lived time form the background against which Proust picks out vivid, discontinuous incidents for description. In the *Search*, the over-all movement of Marcel's life, i.e., time as he ultimately lived it, becomes the figure finally discerned. The ground against which it is gradually revealed consists of all those false scents and misconceptions—the accumulated incidents of the story. The contrast in approach and emphasis is complete, and completely significant for his art. There is another comparison that may illuminate the shift. In "The Circular Ruins" Borges tells the story of a man who discovers that his life consists of, or enacts, the dreams of another more powerful human consciousness, on which he is therefore entirely dependent. Proust "woke up" to the higher consciousness and unity of his literary vision; beside it, or within it, his own life became a dream, a play, a fiction. At this point sheer form becomes an omnivorous force, seeking to assimilate everything it encounters. At this point also, Proust adopted for keeps the ambiguous narrative *I*. He developed a first-person discourse that merges the protagonist of the incidents forming the ground (Marcel) with the retrospective witness-writer (the Narrator) who discovers the figure, the "new form of beauty" superior and exterior to them.

Proust weathered his artistic crisis in mid-career and came out on the other side of it with hopes of making good in three or four years on his big literary wager. In the end he used all fourteen years he had to live. The biography gives a clear enough picture of the outward events, yet it is extremely difficult to speak with certainty about the nature of the insight that transformed Proust's career and produced the *Search*.[17]

In the novel there are two significant differences from the biography. First, Marcel's conversion to literature as a vocation comes not in mid-career as in the case of Proust, but very late—nearly at the end of the book when Marcel is described as an old man. Thus the dramatic effect is enhanced, and the body of the book is constructed as a long decline. My remarks in the previous chapter about art as idolatry and a false scent should suggest how art conforms to that pattern in the *Search*. Painting and music keep some of their savor, but as the story goes on literature, representing Marcel's first aspiration to transcend ordinariness and isolation, withers to a dry husk. Even Marcel's long discussion with Albertine in *The Captive* about Dostoevski, Mme de Sévigné, Thomas Hardy, and Baudelaire, dangles from the troubling thought that "Vinteuil's music seemed

---

[17] Three powerful biographer-critics have approached the subject. In order of increasing judiciousness and mastery of the overwhelming materials, they are: George D. Painter, Henri Bonnet, and Maurice Bardèche.

to me something truer than all known books" (III, 374). These discouragements begin soon after Combray and become one of the leitmotivs of the book until close to the end.[18]

The first difference, then, between the novel and the biography is one of timing. Marcel rediscovers his literary vocation near the end of his life, not in his prime as Proust himself did. The second difference is that what the circumstances of life tend to obscure—namely, the origins and meanings of things—the novel tends to reveal. There lies its essence and its purpose as a work of art. In fact, the earliest sustained reflections on literature in the *Search* develop precisely this esthetic theory.

At the beginning of *Swann's Way* the reader comes upon several celebrated set pieces: the kaleidoscope of bedrooms in Marcel's life; the goodnight kiss withheld and granted; and the *madedeine* dipped in linden tea.

[18] To emphasize this downward movement, Proust wrote a somewhat contrived coda for the last pages of *Swann's Way*, the first volume to be published. The mythological Bois de Boulogne, peopled with the most elegant creatures in the world, collapses into its most paltry self, a mere woods. Six pages of romantic despair lead up to a muted allusion to Horace in the closing lines: ". . . the memory of a certain scene means nothing more than the loss of that instant; and the houses, roads, and avenues are as fleeting, alas, as time itself" (I, 427). The spinning of the story goes on, but deprived now of the hope that memory or art can transcend the flux.

Is it really so? as Proust himself would immediately have asked. In a significant letter written to Jacques Rivière just a few months after publication of *Swann's Way* in 1913, Proust states that this coda is merely "a screen to finish off the volume within the limit of 500 pages" and that the thought expressed there is "the contrary of my conclusion." But at that point in the text, the despair is convincing and authoritative. The weight of the evidence continues to bear it out, not just through a few hundred pages as Proust originally planned, but through five more volumes, before the contrary movement begins in *Time Recaptured*. It makes a prolonged and seemingly irreversible descent.

And what then? Aunt Léonie? The village church and
steeple. The two ways? Each one has high definition.
Yet we cannot go on endlessly dealing with a novel
composed of detachable parts. The pages of "Combray"
form a radial unity that it is unwise to cut up into
scenes and sections. Still, one sequence stands apart
because it casts everything else into doubt and jeopardy.
The Combray world that displays convincing color and
strong personality dims temporarily when seen from
another perspective. The shift occurs when Marcel is
reading in the garden (I, 84–88). This carefully reasoned
yet poetic passage places us suddenly inside his world,
looking out. Marcel's faith in the special world of childhood weakens briefly in the face of a competing faith—
the reality of a book. Art makes the challenge. Marcel
describes his long Sunday afternoons of reading as
forming a single consciousness "simultaneously dappled
with different states." He remains only marginally aware
of the world around him.

> [For] my most intimate thought, the constantly shift-
> ing control that regulated everything else, was my
> belief in the philosophical richness and in the beauty
> of the book I was reading and my desire to appropri-
> ate them for myself (I, 84).

And we are told why. Being not opaque, material creatures but *images*, the characters of such a story are
transparent and can reveal their feelings and motives
to us. As images they can also concentrate the actions
of a lifetime into a few hours' reading, thus making
perceptible what we cannot observe at the slow pace of
living. The transparent image of fiction is doubly revealing compared to life, and hence more alluring than
life. Furthermore, the Narrator explains in this passage,
the "prestige" of the fictional world consoles Marcel for
the apparent mediocrity of his own life and releases
the constant gushing forth [*jaillissement*] of his consciousness toward other things and beings. These beauti-

ful Sunday afternoons, described as "silent, sonorous, perfumed, and limpid," transform Marcel's life and anticipate both the long stretches of soul error and the final return to art. They do not destroy Marcel's basic faith in his childhood experiences, but they shadow it.

As a reader, then, Marcel lives through a few afternoons that both transcend the magic and relieve the mediocrity of childhood. Yet like the impressions and resurrections, they do not last. Instead, they lead into the false or idolatrous attitudes toward art of Swann, Bergotte, Charlus, and Marcel himself. However this first sustained esthetic meditation presents art as a form of revelation and communication that importunes our inmost being. Like the *madeleine* sequence in the domain of memory, it remains a talisman in the domain of art.

Art is never far from the narrative line of the *Search*. Marcel lives surrounded by the mythological presences of art, in the double form of the masterpieces of Western culture and of several characters in the story who practice one of the arts. The three major artists represent a kind of progress: Bergotte, the most compromised by the world, society, and idolatry; Elstir, who seems to work directly with the phenomenon of vision rather than to render reality; and Vinteuil, depicted as a martyr-composer. It is Elstir who means most to Marcel after he has passed adolescence.

> . . . if God the Father created the things of the world by naming them, it is by depriving them of their names, or by giving them new names, that Elstir re-created the world (I, 835).

Marcel gleans lessons like this one and many more along the way. However, such insights become less frequent and more fragmentary with time. Art takes the same downward path as memory. It is not until we are well into the fifth volume that Marcel has another experience of art as intense and as carefully described as the Sunday afternoons in Combray. The fifteen pages devoted to the Vinteuil septet in *The Captive* (III, 248–265) carry Marcel through a series of stations along the path to understanding art. Taken unawares by the music, he first hears it as a description of a seascape, and then associates it with his love for Albertine. After thinking of the piece as an expression of Vinteuil's troubled life, Marcel goes on to discover in the music something "ineffable": a sense of individual being and "the communication of souls" (III, 258). Proust has written a profound meditation on music as a progressive experience engaging one's whole consciousness. The passage is less about music than about coenesthesia, the organic sensation of existence, released by a full encounter with music. Within the context of Marcel's story, however, the incident falls short of changing Marcel's life. He hears the music as a "call" away from the "emptiness" of his life. He cannot answer that call, possibly because he remains a hearer or spectator, possibly because it is a musical rather than a literary experience. Nevertheless, this scene takes so long a step toward divulging the outcome of the novel that Proust saw fit to lead us back into a swamp of misunderstanding and disappointment before the end comes. When Marcel reads the Goncourt brothers' journal (see previous chapter, page 88) he has lost his esthetic bearings so thoroughly that he all but renounces his ambitions as an artist along with his hopes of grasping the significance of past events in his life.

After so many tribulations the outcome of the novel may begin to look strained. When impressions, reminiscences, and art have lost their power to sustain Marcel, how is it that they return miraculously and more compellingly than ever in the long culminating scene? What accounts for this melodramatic turn of events? The basic reason has a sturdy simplicity about it. At long last Marcel comprehends the crucial interrelation between these three elements of his experience. Earlier, he barely associated them. The impressions faded as soon as they occurred. The reminiscences might or might not lead him back to their source among forgotten impressions, and did not reach out toward artistic creation. Art wallowed increasingly in the sloughs of prestige and idolatry. The one exception to this compartmentalization turns up fairly early in the story and is worth a look. I am referring to the scene in "Combray" when Marcel scribbles out on the spot a description of the beautiful slow dance of the Martinville steeples on the horizon as seen from Dr. Percepied's fast moving carriage (I, 178–92). Yet nothing in this carefully composed sequence encourages the reader to regard Marcel's product as a work of art. "I never thought about the page again," the Narrator says. And he ridicules the whole affair by telling us that Marcel began to carry on like "a chicken . . . that had just laid an egg." There is little here to convey any lasting faith in impressions, reminiscences, and art, or to bring them together.

No such flippancy marks the last two hundred pages of the *Search*, even though it contains the great mock-apotheosis of nonrecognition and many smaller comic touches. Five successive resurrections impel Marcel to collect the thoughts and experiences of a lifetime into a final meditation. This philosophical-poetic discourse does not reflect *on* the action at this juncture; its powerful movement of thought *is* the action. It reconstitutes every theme in the novel. Joyce seeks a similar effect in Molly Bloom's great affirmative monologue at the end of *Ulysses*. Marcel's fifty-page monologue that opens the final sequence follows a basic argument as clearly articulated as that of the passage describing the Sunday afternoon readings in Combray. The opposite of a *dénouement*, it knots together the several strands that have hung slack and barely intertwined during the central portion of the novel:

1. Though they bestow a sense of "the essence of things" and of "our true self," resurrections such as those

just experienced by Marcel are of fleeting effect (III, 866–75).

2. The only means to arrest and transfix their elevating impulse is to capture it in a work of art (876–83; 883–88 form a later insertion).

3. The writer does so by creating a metaphorical link or loop between ordinary, lived "reality" and the "vision" of a work of art. This esthetic loop encompasses the analogous loop between past impression and its resurrection in the present (889–96).

4. The understanding of art as a creative process permits Marcel to embrace his literary vocation and to see the carefully defined role literature gives to intelligence and general laws, and to suffering. He also speaks of the role and the rewards of the reader (897–917).

The last two parts of the argument, especially 3, need elucidation.

In approaching what he considers to be the essential function of a work of art, Proust relies heavily on the French word, *rapport*: relation. In the crucial paragraph of his meditation (III, 889), he describes a set of interlocking relations connecting all parts of his universe and based on the "natural" phenomenon of seeing one thing in another through association or analogy. The analogy that links past and present experiences through memory confers on them a sense of "reality," of "true life." Resurrections create a kind of relief or depth perception in time. This reality is in turn related to art through the analogy of metaphor. The transparent, accelerated image of fiction can capture what is opaque or imperceptible in life. Thus art forms a second loop in a different dimension, reaching out of reality and time, yet also flowing back toward them. When Proust describes the writer discovering the *rapport* between art and life, he does so in the context of a now familiar incident.

If I tried to analyze for myself just what takes place in us at the moment when something makes a certain

> impression on us—as, for example, that day when, as I crossed the bridge over the Vivonne, the shadow of a cloud on the water made me exclaim, "Gosh, gosh," as I leaped for joy . . . —I perceived that, to describe these impressions, to write that essential book, the only true book, a great writer does not need to invent it, in the current sense of the term, since it already exists in each one of us, but merely to translate it. The duty and the tasks of a writer are those of a translator (III, 890).

Involuntary memory links past the present into reality. "Translation" links that reality, focused in reminiscences and impressions, to the work of art. A little further on Proust adds a third loop: reading. The reader ultimately reads *himself* in the work of art and gains an insight into his reality by retrospection or anticipation.

In the hope of clarifying my exposition, I have constructed a diagram of the operation of Proust's literary esthetic as I comprehend it (see Diagram VI). The significant aspect of this vision of things is that every element is linked by a universal principle of analogy or relation. Literature, and by implication the other arts, play a key intermediary role between one person's reality and that of another. In fact, the word which best sums up Proust's philosophical attitude in this context, encompassing both an epistemology and an esthetic, is *communication*. In 1905, when toiling to find his way beyond Ruskin's idolatrous attitude toward art, Proust had spoken of reading as "that fecund miracle of communication in the midst of solitude" (*CSB*, 174). For social conversation distracts the mind; solitude strengthens it. Directed toward a work of art, reading brings communication without social distraction. Yet Proust went on to insist that reading constitutes an "incitement" to the true life of the mind, and not the full realization of that life (*ibid.*, 178). Part of the same train of thought reappears in *The Guermantes Way* when the Narrator passes harsh judgment on friendship,

VI. THE LOOPS OF ART

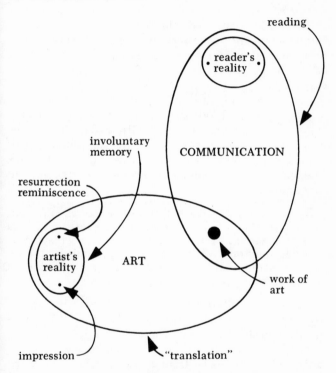

—Any person's experience may emit a field of heightened awareness: namely, *art* in its simplest meaning.

—The pattern central to the *Search* is that of a relationship between a past impression and its resurrection in the present.

—Only the gifted and dedicated artist *translates* his reality into the *work of art*.

—Through the work of art the reader may attain *communication* with others (the artist and, presumably, other readers) and an enhanced recognition of his own lot.

all of whose effort is to make us sacrifice the only part of ourselves which is real and incommunicable (except by means of art) to a superficial self which, unlike the other, finds no reward in its own being (II, 394).

The work of art holds the secret of communication. But at this point in the narrative that truth is confined in a parenthesis of suspended animation, while society carries Marcel along in its distractions. The secret declares itself again during the Vinteuil septet when the ultimate power of music is described as that of allowing us to see "with other eyes," something approaching "the communication of souls" (III, 258). One of the most expansive passages in the last meditation leaves little doubt that art provides the antidote to Proust's complaint, to the solitary confinement of the human condition.

By art alone can we get out of ourselves, find out what another person sees of this universe which is not the same as ours. . . . Thanks to art, instead of seeing only one world, we see it multiplied, and we have as many different worlds at our disposition as there are original artists (III, 895–96).

Proust rarely allowed himself such flights when speaking specifically about literature. In the following pages the communication a book affords, its incitement, is compared to that of an optical instrument which "the author offers the reader in order to allow him to discern things which, without the book, he would possibly not have seen in himself. The reader's recognition in himself of what the book says is proof of the book's truth, and vice versa" (III, 911). True reading of a worthwhile book takes us just far enough out of ourselves and our solitude to return to them restored. Art affords this communication with our own life through self-recognition. Those admirers of art who cannot make the return trip to their own reality are harshly judged by Proust as "*célibataires* of art" (III, 892). Their admiration has no dynamic relation to their own lives. Permanently sensitized by Ruskin, Proust would never allow art to present itself as a substitute for life, even for the life of the mind, but only as the exercise of communication which leads us back into life. When Marcel's Sunday afternoon reading in Combray tempted him to turn away from his existence in dissatisfaction and desire, he was misusing art as an escape and not discerning himself through its lens. In a boy this is natural enough. It may take the better part of a lifetime to discover that reading can augment rather than diminish one's own life and circumstances.

In sum, art springs from life and in turn serves it through the interlocking *rapports* or loops of communication. Yet there remains an underlying inconsistency between this affirmation that art belongs to life and Proust's thoughts on solitude and society. Everything he says about social life and friendship and snobbery as contrasted to reading and meditation establishes the vanity of social intercourse next to the true rewards of solitude. To converse with a friend is "a self-abdication" (II, 906). Marcel prefers to read and look at pictures alone; on country walks he drops behind his friends when he wants to commune with a hawthorn bush or a view of the ocean. The deepest experiences of memory and art appear to be excluded from that portion of our lives spent with other people. Few divisions in Proust's universe go so deep as this cleavage between the integrity of solitude, associated with memory and art, and the distraction of society associated with superficiality and snobbery.[19]

[19] During the *madeleine* resurrection, Marcel's mother is with him and in fact supplies both the tea and the cake. However, the text does not indicate that she either shares the experience or receives an account of it from her son. He becomes totally rapt in his own mental processes and never mentions her again even at the end of the sequence. It is significant that during the Martinville steeples impression,

Yet the close of the book brings an unexpected shift in Marcel's attitude. Most of the dramatic developments at the end, concerning art and memory and vocation, have been anticipated many times over in earlier passages. But on the matter of society and solitude, Marcel and the Narrator have kept their secrets of state very successfully. Directly after the fifty-page meditation on the nature of art and its relation to memory and to life, Marcel is told that he can enter the salon and join the other guests. Brought back to himself and his surroundings, he seems to have found a new calm.

> But in the line of thought upon which I was embarked I was not in the least disturbed by the fact that a fashionable gathering, my return to society, might have provided me with that point of departure for a new life which I had been unable to find in solitude. There was nothing extraordinary about this fact, there was no reason why an impression with the power to resuscitate the timeless man within me should be linked to solitude rather than to society (as I had once supposed and as had perhaps once been the case, and as perhaps would still have had to be the case had I developed harmoniously instead of going through this long period of arrest which seemed only now to be coming to an end) . . . I felt that the impulse given to the intellectual life within me was so vigorous now that I would be able to pursue these thoughts just as well in the drawing room, in the midst of the guests, as alone in the library; it seemed to me that, from this point of view, even in the midst of a numerous gathering, I would be able to maintain my solitude (III, 918).

Undistracted, no longer deceived by the false prestige of noble names and celebrated faces, sustained by the sense of his own life as worth living, Marcel passes

---

the coachman, next to whom Marcel was sitting, refused to talk with him. ". . . I was obliged, for lack of any other company, to fall back on myself" (I, 180).

among the guests and watches the scene around him as if it were part of a play or a painting. Marcel here achieves the familiarity and the detachment to behold these other people without soul error, without the abdication of self that has always beset him before in a social context. His equanimity and powers of recognition allow him at last to enter into his own existence as into a work of art, briefly transcending intermittence by fusing solitude and social intercourse. Marcel can now return safely and even profitably to his old haunts. What ensues is a magnificent comic scene revealing the tenacity of general and individual human traits beneath the grotesque masquerade of age. Odette and the Prince de Guermantes and the rest are incorrigibly themselves to their last breath—which seems very near.

Presumably Marcel could now find the rewards of old age in the same social milieu that for years arrested his development. Yet it is not to be so. Marcel the writer realizes that he must devote the months remaining to him to composing the book he feels alive within him as the true fruit of his experience. Having attained an inner equilibrium of solitude and society, he will not have time to enjoy it. It is the final irony. Attended only by Françoise, Marcel must turn resolutely to his solitary work as an artist.[20]

Even though it opens a place for the reader, Proust's esthetic raises an uncomfortable question: is full salvation by art reserved for the creative artist? The three major artists in the book play the role of collective godfather to Marcel. Until he finds his own vocation, they

[20] In *Proust's Binoculars*, I consider two important aspects of Proust's esthetic which are omitted here. One is the way in which the topographical division of Combray into "two ways" resolves finally into one and becomes a metaphor for metaphor itself (pp. 125–27). The other concerns the double, twice-lived nature of life, for whose total experience literature cannot substitute. But literature can furnish one beat of that double rhythm of re-cognition and thus modify the basic economy of living (pp. 132–36).

take his vows for him and guide him on his way. Conversely, the gifted amateurs—Swann, Charlus, even his grandmother—are all "bachelors of art" and often lead him astray. When Marcel comes back to art at an advanced age, he does so not as an amateur or appreciative spectator but as a novelist. The hierarchy of functions is fully declared. Yet there are a few glints of hope for the nonartist and ordinary citizen. The basic materials of art, meaning impressions and possibly reminiscences, exist in all of us, available for translation into art. The true text is life itself, if only we know how to approach it. Art is a matter of vision and revision. A few pages later Proust develops this thought and dramatically closes the loops between life and literature. Realism depicts only the surface of things, he states; both and life and art lie "underneath."

> The greatness of true art . . . was to find, grasp, and bring out that reality which we live at a great distance from . . . that reality which we run the risk of dying without having known, and which is quite simply our own life. True life, life finally discovered and illuminated, is literature; that life which, in a sense, at every moment inhabits all men as well as the artist (III, 895).

"All men" does not equivocate; "in a sense" holds something back. The stuff of literature is there for all to find and take. Few people find it; fewer still translate it into a work of art. But it is precisely that literary work which may help the less gifted to find their true life. They do so not vicariously by seeking to identify with another life, but indirectly by the reciprocating movement of literature, which propels them first toward clearly visible beings in a novel and then back toward their own existence insofar as they recognize themselves in the story. But only the writer-artist has the task and the reward of extruding a work of art out of his own experience. According to Proust's mature esthetic, which is also his ethic, the writer draws both on an exceptional memory (encompassing impressions and reminiscences) and on a logical-imaginative insight which related these mnemonic experiences to, and in, the work of art—process and product as one. The shape and the content of the *Search* derive from this esthetic insight. The novel depicts the artist very much in the role of the Prodigal Son, or of Ulysses. After a long journey and many trials, a joyful homecoming. It is primarily the obbligato motifs of suffering and work in the artist's life that keep the conclusion from sounding prideful. Within that obbligato, furthermore, one detects the soft but unmistakable suggestion that each one of us is potentially the artist of his own life.

APPENDIX

In the fall of 1912 Proust thought he had virtually finished his novel. Half of it was in typescript, half still in manuscript. After submitting the first half to the publisher Fasquelle, he decided that he might do better with the new house set up by the *Nouvelle Revue Française*. Through friends he sent another copy of the typescript to Jacques Copeau, André Gide, and Jean Schlumberger, the *NRF* editors, accompanied by a long statement explaining the purpose and methods of his novel. Principally on the basis of Gide's hasty judgment, they turned him down a month later in a now famous decision they soon came to regret.

A few days before Grasset finally published *Swann's Way* in November 1913, Proust arranged for *Le Temps* to run an interview with him. Elie-Joseph Bois, the journalist who visited Proust for the purpose, received a copy of the statement originally written for the *NRF* editors the year before. He reproduced it virtually unchanged, adding his own comments as an opening. Thus the interview contains both one of the earliest published descriptions of Proust's living conditions and his most coherent and cogent declaration of artistic faith at that period. Many of its themes and phrases are borrowed directly from portions of the novel that would not appear for several years.

The complete text has not previously been translated into English.

In Search of Lost Time
—Elie-Joseph Bois

This is the enigmatic title of a novel the first volume of which has just appeared and has provoked much curiosity. A few pages of it have already passed from hand to hand, and those privileged readers speak of the book with great enthusiasm. Such premature success is often an advantage, and sometimes a hidden danger. I do not know how public opinion will react in this case, whether it will consecrate as a masterpiece, as some have already called it, this self-contained opening volume entitled *Swann's Way*. But I run no risk in predicting that it will leave no reader indifferent. It will probably disconcert many readers. *Swann's Way* is not a book to read on the train, skipping over the pages with one eye on the landscape; it is a book of true originality and profundity to the point of strangeness, claiming the reader's full attention and even seizing it forcibly. Its clutch takes you by surprise; it confuses and overwhelms. As for plot—plot in the sense of what we rely on in most novels to carry us along in some state of expectation through a series of adventures to the necessary resolution—there just is no such thing here. There is an action of sorts, but its threads seem to be covered over with an exaggerated concern for discretion, and it is up to us to find our own way through, breathing heavily, absorbed in the development of characters which the author etches pitilessly in successive situations. A novel of analysis, yes; but I know of few novels in which the analysis penetrates so deep. At times you want to cry out, "Enough!" as to a surgeon who spares no detail in describing an operation. Yet you never say it. You keep on turning the pages feverishly in order to see further into the souls of these creatures. What you see is a certain Swann in love with Odette de Crécy, and how his love changes into an anxious, suspicious, unhealthy passion tormented by the most atrocious jealousy. You probably know the kind. It happens in every novel, in every play, on every street corner. But in this case we aren't kept on the outside of things; willy-nilly we are thrust into the mind and heart and body of that man. An impassive guide leads us on and forces us to look, to read each thought, to live each emotion, from the joy of spreading happiness to the pangs of jealousy that rack the heart and leave one's head in a whirl. The same thing happens with a child's love for his mother, and with a boy's puppy love for one of his playmates, and with all the characters' feelings in *Swann's Way*.

Mr. Marcel Proust is the author of this disturbing book.

The translator and critic of Ruskin is by no means unknown to the reading public. Mr. Anatole France, toward whom he feels deep gratitude, wrote the preface for *Pleasures and Days*, a charming work whose extreme indecency Mr. Proust regrets (the word is his own) but does not disavow. The older author characterized him as a depraved Bernardin de Saint-Pierre and an innocent Petronius. Mr. Edouard Rod found in him an affinity to La Bruyère. Mr. Albert Sorel gave an account of his first book in this newspaper. After that, except for an occasional article, Mr. Proust withdrew within himself, or rather illness forced him to withdraw. It is no new writer, then, who comes along today to offer us *Swann's Way*. In *Pleasures and Days* there's already a preliminary version, called *Jealousy's End*, of the most striking

chapter in the new novel. In the preface to his translation of *Sesame and Lilies*, you will find the embryo of
another chapter. But the writer has undergone a great
change, His horizons have broadened, and at the same
time his sensibility has matured to the point where he
can say: "There's not a single adjective in my new work
that's not fully felt." Like plants which grow best in a
hothouse, Mr. Marcel Proust, intent upon himself, has
drawn out of his own suffering a creative energy demon-
strated in his novel. He set himself a task. But what
task? He can describe it better than I can.

Mr. Marcel Proust is lying down in a bedroom whose
shutters are almost permanently closed. Electric light
accentuates the dull color of his face, but two fine eyes
burning with life and fever gleam below the hair that
falls over his forehead. Mr. Marcel Proust is still the
slave of his illness, but that person disappears when the
writer, invited to comment on his work, comes to life
and begins to talk.

"I'm publishing only one volume, *Swann's Way*, of a
multivolume novel which will have the general title,
In Search of Lost Time. I would have liked to publish
the whole work together, but these days editors won't
bring out several volumes at a time. I feel like someone
with a tapestry too large for any of his rooms and who
has to cut it up into sections.

"Many young writers, with whom I'm on good terms,
favor the opposite course: short action, few characters.
That's not my conception of the novel. I'll try to explain
why. As you know we have both plane and solid geometry—geometry in two-dimensional and in three-dimen-
sional space. Well, for me the novel means not just
plane (or plain) psychology but psychology in time. It is
this invisible substance of time that I have tried to isolate, and it meant that the experiment had to last over
a long period. I hope that at the end of my book certain
unimportant social events, like the marriage between

two characters who in the first volume belonged to totally different social worlds, will imply that time has passed and will take on the kind of beauty and patina you can see on the statues at Versailles which time has gradually coated with an emerald sheath.

"Then, like a city which, from a train following its winding track, appears first on one side of the car and then on the other, the various situations in which one character will have been seen by another—to the point of seeming to be different and successive characters instead of the same one—will give, and for that very reason, the sensation of time elapsed. Some characters will turn out later quite different from what they are in the present volume, different from what we think they are, as it happens in life."

Mr. Proust told us that it is not just certain characters that will reappear with modifications, as in cycles of Balzac's novels. Certain profound, almost unconscious impressions will recur in the same person. And he went on.

"From this point of view, my book might be seen as an attempt at a series of 'novels of the unconscious.' I would not be ashamed to say 'Bergsonian novels' if I believed it, for in every age literature tries to find a link—after the fact, of course—to the reigning philosophy. But the term would be inaccurate, for my work is based on the distinction between involuntary and voluntary memory, a distinction which not only does not appear in Mr. Bergson's philosophy, but is even contradicted by it."

"How do you make this distinction?"

"To my way of thinking, voluntary memory, which belongs above all to the intelligence and the eyes, offers us only untruthful aspects of the past; but if an odor or a taste, re-encountered in totally different circumstances, unexpectedly reawakens the past in us, then we can sense how different this past was from what we thought we could remember, from what voluntary memory ofered us, like a painter working with false colors. Already, in the first volume, you will see the character who tells the story, and who says 'I' (he's not me), suddenly rediscover forgotten times, forgotten gardens and people, in the taste of a sip of tea with a *madeleine* cake soaked in it. Probably he could remember these things, but without any vividness or attraction; I was able to have him say that, as in the Japanese trick of dropping into a bowl of water tiny bits of paper which then unfurl and fill out into flowers and people, all the flowers in his garden, and the Vivonne water lilies, and the good folk of the village along with their houses and their church, and the whole of Combray and its environs, all that, with its shape and solidity restored, comes forth, town and gardens, from his cup of tea.

"So you see, I believe that the writer should expect involuntary memory to furnish almost all the raw material of his work. First of all, precisely because such memories are involuntary, because they take shape of their own accord out of the attraction of one moment or another, they alone carry the seal of authenticity. Second, they bring things back in the right proportion of memory and forgetfulness. Finally, since they let us experience the same sensation in a totally different setting, they liberate it from all contingency and give us its extratemporal essence, the essence which becomes the content of meaningful style, the general and necessary truth which beauty of style alone can express.

"I'm talking this way about my book," Mr. Proust went on, "because I have in no way written a work of reasoning, because all its elements have been furnished by my sensibility, because I first perceived them deep within me without understanding them, and have had as much difficulty putting them into intelligible form as if they were alien to the intelligence, like a musical theme. You may think I'm talking about extreme subleties. Not at all, believe me, but about realities. Anything we have not had to elucidate ourselves, anything that

was clear before we came along (logical ideas, for ex
ample), does not really belong to us, we don't even
know if it's real. We choose arbitrarily from 'the possi
ble.' Anyway, you know, you can see all this in the style

"Style has nothing to do with embellishment, as some
people think; it's not even a matter of technique. Like
the color sense in some painters, it's a quality of vision,
the revelation of the particular universe that each of us
sees and that no one else sees. The pleasure an artist
offers us is to convey another universe to us."

In that case, we ask, how is it that some writers
claim to have no style at all? Mr. Proust cannot understand them and insists:

"They could say that only if they have given up trying
to get to the bottom of their impressions."

Mr. Proust has dedicated *Swann's Way* "To Mr. Gaston
Calmette, as an expression of deep and affectionate
gratitude."

"I may have older debts," Mr. Proust told us, "toward
masters to whom I have dedicated works written before
this one but which will appear after it—first of all to
Anatole France, who treated me practically like a son.
Thanks to Mr. Calmette, I experienced the joy of a
young man who reads his first published article.

"And also," Mr. Proust added with a note of melan-
choly, "since publication of my articles in his newspaper
gave me a way of visiting certain people I found it hard
to do without, he helped me make the change from a
social to a solitary life . . ."

And the gesture made by this ailing author brought
me back to the darkened room with its closed shutters,
where the sun never enters. But his look shows no sad-
ness. If the invalid has reason to complain, the writer
has reason to be proud. The latter has consoled the
former.

Le Temps
13 November, 1913

ACKNOWLEDGMENTS

A travel grant from the American Philosophical Society, Philadelphia, Pennsylvania, permitted me to consult the collection of Proust manuscripts in the Bibliothèque Nationale, Paris.

Some materials in this book were originally presented in a series of three lectures during November 1971 at the University of Wisconsin, Madison, as part of a symposium celebrating the Proust centenary and sponsored by the Department of Romance Languages; and in the John Hamilton Fulton Memorial Lecture at Middlebury College, Vermont, in January 1973.

A modified version of a section from Chapter IV is included in the essay "This Must Be the Place: from Wordsworth to Proust," in *Romanticism: Vistas, Distances, Continuities*, eds. David Thorburn and Geoffrey Hartman. Ithaca: Cornell University Press, 1973.

R. S.

SHORT BIBLIOGRAPHY

See page vii for the standard edition in French of Proust's works and for the editions in English of *In Search of Lost Time* (published title: *Remembrance of Things Past*).

Proust's correspondence, originally collected in six volumes during the 1930s and supplemented in numerous separate collections since then, is now being consolidated and re-edited by Philip Kolb. The first two volumes have appeared (Paris: Plon, 1970, 1973).

I. ENGLISH TRANSLATIONS OF WORKS OTHER THAN *In Search of Lost Time*

Marcel Proust: A selection from His Miscellaneous Writings. Trans. Gerard Hopkins. London: Allan Wingate, 1948.

The Maxims of Marcel Proust. Ed. and trans. Justin O'Brien. New York: Columbia University Press, 1948.

Letters of Marcel Proust. Selected and trans. Minna Curtiss. New York: Random House, 1949.

Jean Santeuil. Trans. Gerard Hopkins. New York: Simon & Schuster, 1956.

Pleasures and Days and Other Writings. Trans. Louise Varèse, Gerard Hopkins, and Barbara Dupee; ed. F. W. Dupee. Garden City, N. Y.: Anchor Books, 1957.

Marcel Proust: Letters to His Mother. Trans. George D. Painter. New York: Citadel Press, 1957.

Marcel Proust on Art and Literature, 1896–1919. Trans. Sylvia Townsend Warner. New York: Meridian, 1958 (Contains *Against Sainte-Beuve* in the extended text published by Gallimard in 1954.)

On Reading. Trans. Jean Autret and William Burford. New York: Macmillan, 1971. A bilingual edition of Proust's Preface to his own translation, published in 1906, of Ruskin's *Sesame and Lilies.*

I. ON PROUST AND HIS WORK

In the lists below an asterisk indicates a work containing useful bibliography.

. *Books of a general nature and biographies*

arker, Richard H. *Marcel Proust: a Biography.* New York: Criterion, 1958.

Bersani, Jacques, ed. *Les Critiques de notre temps et Proust.* Paris: Garnier, 1971.

Brée, Germaine. *The World of Marcel Proust.* Boston: Houghton Mifflin, 1966.

Fowlie, Wallace. *A Reading of Proust.* Garden City, N. Y.: Anchor Books, 1964.

indus, Milton. *The Proustian Vision.* New York: Columbia University Press, 1954.

evin, Harry. *The Gates of Horn: A Study of Five French Realists.* New York: Oxford University Press, 1963. (Chapter VII is on Proust.)

Maurois, André. *A la recherche de Marcel Proust.* Paris: Hachette, 1949. (*Proust, Portrait of a Genius.* Gerard Hopkins, trans. New York: Harper, 1950.)

Painter, George D. *Proust: the Early Years* and *Proust: the Later Years.* 2 vols. Boston: Atlantic-Little Brown, 1959, 1965.

oulet, Georges. *Etudes sur le temps humain.* Paris: Plon, 1949. (Chapter on Proust.) (*Studies in Human Time.* Elliot Coleman, trans. Baltimore: Johns Hopkins University Press, 1956.)

Tadié, J.-Y. ed. *Lectures de Proust.* Paris: Armand Colin, 1971.

. *Other works mentioned in the text*

ardèche, Maurice. *Proust romancier.* 2 vols. Paris: Les Sept Couleurs, 1971.

éhar, Serge. *L'Univers médical de Proust* (Cahiers Marcel Proust, nouvelle série, I). Paris: Gallimard, 1970.

ersani, Leo. *Marcel Proust: the Fictions of Life and of Art.* New York: Oxford University Press, 1965.

Brée, Germaine. *Du temps perdu au temps retrouvé.* Paris: Les Belles Lettres, 1950. (*Marcel Proust and Deliverance from Time.* C. J. Richards and A. D. Truitt, trans. New Brunswick, N.J.: Rutgers University Press, 1955.)

*Bonnet, Henri. *Marcel Proust de 1907 à 1914.* Paris: Nizet, 1971.

Deleuze, Gilles. *Proust et les signes.* 2ᵉ ed. Paris: P. U. F., 1970. (*Proust and Signs.* Richard Howard, trans. Paperback. New York: George Braziller, 1972.)

Fernandez, Dominique. *L'Arbre jusqu'aux racines.* Paris: Grasset, 1972.

Frank, Joseph. *The Widening Gyre.* New Brunswick: Rutgers University Press, 1963.

Genette, Gérard. *Figures I, II, III.* Paris: Seuil, 1966, 1969, 1973.

Girard, René. *Mensonge romantique et vérité romanesque.* Paris: Grasset, 1961. (*Deceit, Desire, and the Novel: Self and Other in Literary Structure.* Y. Freccero, trans. Baltimore: Johns Hopkins University Press, 1966.)

Muller, Marcel. *Les Voix narratives dans "A la recherche du temps perdu."* Geneva: Droz, 1965.

Picon, Gaëtan. *Lecture de Proust.* Paris: Mercure de France, 1963.

Pierre-Quint, Léon. *Marcel Proust.* Paris: Sagittaire, 1935.

Poulet, Georges. *L'Espace proustien.* Paris: Gallimard, 1963.

Revel, J.-F. *Sur Proust.* Paris: Julliard, 1960. (*On Proust.* Martin Turnell, trans. Paperback. LaSalle, Ill.: Open Court, 1973.)

Rousset, Jean. *Forme et signification.* Paris: Corti, 1962.

Shattuck, Roger. *Proust's Binoculars.* New York: Random House, 1963.

Stambolian, George. *Marcel Proust and the Creative Encounter.* Chicago: University of Chicago Press, 1972.

Wilson, Edmund. *Axel's Castle.* New York: Scribner's, 1931.

Zaehner, R. C. *Mysticism, Sacred and Profane.* New York: Oxford University Press, 1957.

Valuable essays on Proust have been written by Roland Barthes, Samuel Beckett, Walter Benjamin, Maurice Blanchot, Michel Butor, Ernst Robert Curtius, José Ortega y Gasset, Jacques Rivière, Jean-Paul Sartre, Leo Spitzer, and Paul Valéry.

INDEX